"ALL THE REAL INDIANS DIED OFF"

AND 20 OTHER MYTHS ABOUT NATIVE AMERICANS

ROXANNE DUNBAR-ORTIZ
AND DINA GILIO-WHITAKER

BEACON PRESS
BOSTON

BEACON PRESS
Boston, Massachusetts
www.beacon.org

Beacon Press books
are published under the auspices of
the Unitarian Universalist Association of Congregations.

19 18 17 16   8 7 6 5 4 3 2

This book is printed on acid-free paper that meets the uncoated paper
ANSI/NISO specifications for permanence as revised in 1992.

Text design and composition by Kim Arney

Portions of myth 17, "Indians Are Anti-Science," are reprinted
from Dina Gilio-Whitaker, "5 Things You Didn't Think of as Native
Technology," Indian Country Today Media Network, June 30, 2015,
http://indiancountrytodaymedianetwork.com/.

Library of Congress Cataloging-in-Publication Data
Names: Dunbar-Ortiz, Roxanne, author. I Gilio-Whitaker, Dina, author.
Title: "All the real Indians died off" : and 20 other myths about Native
    Americans / Roxanne Dunbar-Ortiz and Dina Gilio-Whitaker.
Description: Boston, Massachusetts : Beacon Press, 2016.
Identifiers: LCCN 2016003644 I ISBN 978-0-8070-6265-4 (paperback) I
    ISBN 978-0-8070-6266-1 (e-book)
Subjects: LCSH: Indians of North America—Historiography. I BISAC: SOCIAL
    SCIENCE / Ethnic Studies / Native American Studies. I HISTORY /
    Native American.
Classification: LCC E76.8 .D85 2016 I DDC 970.004/97—dc23
LC record available at http://lccn.loc.gov/2016003644

"In her in-depth and intelligent analysis of US history from the Indigenous perspective, Roxanne Dunbar-Ortiz challenges readers to rethink the myth that Indian lands were free lands and that genocide was a justifiable means to a glorious end. A must-read for anyone interested in the truth behind this nation's founding and its often contentious relationship with Indigenous peoples."

—Veronica E. Velarde Tiller,
PhD, Jicarilla Apache author, historian,
and publisher of *Tiller's Guide to Indian Country*

"*An Indigenous Peoples' History of the United States* provides an essential historical reference for all Americans. Particularly, it serves as an indispensable text for students of all ages to advance their appreciation and greater understanding of our history and our rightful place in America. The American Indians' perspective has been absent from colonial histories for too long, leaving continued misunderstandings of our struggles for sovereignty and human rights."

—Peterson Zah,
former president of the Navajo Nation

"In this riveting book, Roxanne Dunbar-Ortiz decolonizes American history and illustrates definitively why the past is never very far from the present. Exploring the borderlands between action and narration, between what happened and what is said to have happened, Dunbar-Ortiz strips us of our forged innocence, shocks us into new awarenesses, and draws a straight line from the sins of our fathers—settler-colonialism, the doctrine of discovery, the myth of manifest destiny, white supremacy, theft, and systematic killing—to the contemporary condition of permanent war, invasion and occupation, mass incarceration, and the constant use and threat of state violence. Best of all, she points a way beyond amnesia, paralyzing guilt, or helplessness toward discovering our deepest humanity in a project of truth-telling and repair. *An Indigenous Peoples' History of the United States* will forever change the way we read history and understand our own responsibility to it."

—Bill Ayers

"Roxanne Dunbar-Ortiz's *An Indigenous Peoples' History of the United States* should be essential reading in schools and colleges. It pulls up the paving stones and lays bare the deep history of the United States, from the corn to the reservations. If the United States is a 'crime scene,' as she calls it, then Dunbar-Ortiz is its forensic scientist. A sobering look at a grave history."

—Vijay Prashad,
author of *The Poorer Nations*

"This may well be the most important US history book you will read in your lifetime. If you are expecting yet another 'new' and improved historical narrative or synthesis of Indians in North America, think again. Instead Roxanne Dunbar-Ortiz radically reframes US history, destroying all foundation myths to reveal a brutal settler-colonial structure and ideology designed to cover its bloody tracks. Here, rendered in honest, often poetic words, is the story of those tracks and the people who survived—bloodied but unbowed. Spoiler alert: the colonial era is still here, and so are the Indians."

—Robin D. G. Kelley,
author of *Freedom Dreams*

"ALL THE REAL INDIANS DIED OFF"

To the memory of John Trudell (1946–2015),
who ceaselessly committed his life to the shattering
of Native American myths through poetry and music

Contents

Authors' Note

This book started out as a solo project with Roxanne as the sole author, coming on the heels of the release of her previous book, *An Indigenous Peoples' History of the United States*. With the book enjoying so much success, Roxanne found herself with months of a demanding travel schedule, doing public speaking engagements to promote the book. Taking on a coauthor seemed like the expedient and smart thing to do. Knowing of Dina's work as an award-winning journalist, speaker, and expert in Native American studies, Roxanne asked if Dina was available for the task. For Dina, as a first-time author, having a book deal handed to her was a dream come true. It was a perfect scenario all the way around. Coauthoring this book together has been delightful.

A book like this comes from years of academic training, research, and writing. Between the two of us coauthors, there is well over half a century of formal education, learning, mentoring, knowledge, and activism. It also comes from those who provided influence along the way. That includes all of the family members and friends, professors, teaching assistants, mentors, counselors, colleagues, librarians, and various others who provide the support—in all its myriad forms—that it takes to be an academic, be it a student, professor, department chair, or research associate. Every person who was there on our journey has in some small or big way contributed to this book. That's a lot of people.

But such a book comes from more than just working with influential people, having academic training, and knowing the most current theoretical and pedagogical trends in the fields of history, Native American studies, American studies, and all the other disciplines that feed into them. Yes, the academic background is necessary. But knowing and being able to articulate clearly what all the most prevalent myths and stereotypes about Native Americans are comes at least as much from the lived experience of being Native, in its infinite manifestations. As we discuss throughout these pages, this knowledge inevitably includes processes of inclusion and exclusion and personal histories of profound cultural loss, things neither of us are strangers to. To know personally the myths and stereotypes about Indians is to grow up hearing the narratives behind those myths, knowing that they were lies being told about you and your family and that you were expected to explain yourself at the demands of others.

That lived Native experience, however, is also about reclamation. For us as scholars it is reclaiming stolen pasts through scholarship, storytelling, relationship building, and acknowledging our ancestry. We are who we are because of the ancestors who walked before us, those who suffered and died because of who they were. They gave us special gifts, and we say *lem lempt*—thank you—to them for giving us life.

Finally, this book is born out of the belief that another world is possible when enough people understand how the miseducation about history contributes to the maintenance of systems of social injustice. We believe that people are hungry for a more accurate history and eager to abandon the misperceptions that result in racism toward American Indians. The dehumanization of one is the dehumanization of all. This book is therefore a call to action to envision a better future for everyone, Indian and non-Indian alike.

A NOTE ON TERMINOLOGY

Authors writing from an Indigenous perspective often find the need to contextualize and clarify the terms of choice when writing for a general audience. This is due to much confusion about the correct terms for Native Americans, a topic we devote an entire chapter to. As we note in myth 20, most common terms are problematic, but we both grew up in an era before the word "Indian" came to be seen as pejorative, and most Native people today do not object to the word. Thus we use the terms "Indian," "Indigenous," "Native American," and "Native" interchangeably but defer to specific nation names whenever possible. We avoid the terms "tribe" and "tribal" whenever possible because of their historical association with an ideology of inferiority, and we privilege instead the term "nations." For this reason we also integrate the term "Fourth World" (which we define in myth 1) to emphasize the geopolitical nature of Indigenous peoples.

INTRODUCTION

It is quite possible that war is the continuation of
politics by another means, but isn't politics itself
a continuation of war by other means?

—Michel Foucault[1]

No collectivity of people in US American society is as enigmatic or misunderstood as Indigenous peoples. From the very first encounters with them five centuries ago, Europeans were confounded by these peoples who looked so different and lived lives that seemed not just diametrically opposed to theirs but even blasphemous. Europeans brought with them their fears and prejudices accompanied by a sense of entitlement to the land that had been home to the Indigenous peoples for untold thousands of years. They were occasionally respected by the newcomers, some of whom voluntarily left their own communities in the early days of settlement to live among the Indians. They learned to speak the Natives' languages, intermarried, and had children with them, sometimes for love or companionship, sometimes just to build alliances and gain access to Native territories and to convert them to Christianity. But by and large the history of relations between Indigenous and settler is fraught with conflict, defined by a struggle for land, which is inevitably a struggle for power and control. Five hundred years later, Native peoples are still fighting to protect their lands and their rights to exist as distinct political communities and individuals.

Most US citizens' knowledge about Indians is inaccurate, distorted, or limited to elementary-school textbooks, cheesy old spaghetti westerns, or more contemporary films like *Dances with Wolves* or *The Last of the Mohicans*. Few can name more than a handful of Native nations out of the over five hundred that still exist or can tell you who Leonard Peltier is. Mention Indian gaming and they will have strong opinions about it one way or another. Some might even have an Indian casino in their community, but they will probably be curiously incurious if you ask them how Indian gaming came to be or about the history of the nation that owns the casino. In many parts of the country it's not uncommon for non-Native people to have never met a Native person or to assume that there are no Indians who live among them. On the other hand, in places where there is a concentration of Natives, like in reservation border towns, what non-Native people think they know about Indians is typically limited to racist tropes about drunk or lazy Indians. They are seen as people who are maladjusted to the modern world and cannot free themselves from their tragic past.

On the whole, it can be said that the average US citizen's knowledge about American Indians is confined to a collection of well-worn myths and half-truths that have Native people either not existing at all or existing in a way that fails to live up to their expectations about who "real" Indians are. If Indians do exist, they are seen as mere shadows of their former selves, making counterfeit identity claims or performing fraudulent acts of Indianness that are no longer authentic or even relevant. Non-Natives thus position themselves, either wittingly or unwittingly, as being the true experts about Indians and their histories—and it happens at all levels of society, from the uneducated all the way up to those with advanced college degrees, and even in the halls of Congress. The result is the perpetual erasure of Indians from the US political and cultural landscape.

In short, for five centuries Indians have been disappearing in the collective imagination. They are disappearing in plain sight. The myths about Indigenous peoples that this book identifies can be traced to narratives of erasure. They have had—and continue to have—a profoundly negative impact on the lives of the millions of Native people who still live on the continent of their ancient ancestors. They work further to keep non-Natives in a state of ignorance, forever misinformed and condemned to repeat the mistakes of history, silently eroding their own humanity when they fail to recognize their roles in—or, more specifically, the ways they benefit from—the ongoing injustice of a colonial system. For Native people the effects are felt at every level of personal and public life. They play out in a dizzying array of overt and subtly bigoted ways, resulting in what social scientists call "structural violence." Structural violence describes social arrangements that cause harm to people as they are embedded in the social and political structures of society.[2] It can be so blatant that it manifests in acts of individual physical violence, but it can just as easily result in harm by neglect. Erasure is one of the more subtle forms of structural violence visited upon Native peoples.

At a cultural level, structural violence shows up in dehumanizing portrayals of caricaturized images of Indians in the name of honor and respect. This is most obvious in the stubborn adherence to Indian sports mascots, as in the case of Dan Snyder's Washington Redsk*ns team name. It is also visible in cultural appropriations such as the ubiquitous (and seemingly harmless) Indian Halloween costumes and feather headdresses worn at music festivals or by models for fashion layouts and runway displays. Cultural appropriation is especially egregious when it involves the co-optation of spiritual ceremonies and the inappropriate use of lands deemed sacred by Native peoples. The New Age movement is a Pandora's box full of examples of what has been called the plastic or white shaman.[3] Misuse of sacred land has a long history, and it continues. In 2015, Lakota people in South Dakota protested the annual hippie Rainbow Family gathering in the sacred Paha Sapa (Black Hills). The Lakota claimed that these gatherings have a long history of destructive land use and also cited Rainbow Family drug culture, which they saw as highly disrespectful in a place they believe to be the heart and origin of their people.

Popular culture has a long history of portraying stereotyped and blatantly racist images of American Indians, especially in film. Cree filmmaker Neil Diamond's documentary *Reel Injuns* traces the history of Indians in Hollywood movies, identifying images we are all too familiar with. With roots in the "vanishing Indian" era of late nineteenth and early twentieth century history, Hollywood filmmakers (like other photo-documentarians of the time such as Edward Curtis) rushed to capture images of Indians before they disappeared into the mists of the past. Throughout each era of the twentieth century, Indians appeared in films as literal projections of non-Natives' fantasies about Indians. They include the tragically vanishing Indian, the mystic warrior, the noble and ignoble savage, and eventually the "groovy injun," embodied as the environmental Indian (the iconic crying "Indian," Iron Eyes Cody), the civil rights fighter (*Billy Jack*), and others.[4]

Structural violence against Native people often entails a staggering assortment of legislation, court cases, executive decisions, and municipal and state actions that directly affect their lives. This sort of violence will be explored throughout this book, but one of the most potent ways that violence of erasure is deployed in US society is through education. A body of scholarship identifies the ways that Native children have for generations been miseducated under deliberately repressive federal policy, and a substantial body of research also identifies the ways children in public schools are miseducated on US and Native history.[5] Education scholar Timothy Lintner writes, "History is a delicate amalgam of fact and fiction tempered by personal and pedagogical perception. Though the premise of history is rooted in empiricism, the teaching of history is not so subjective. History classrooms are not neutral; they are contested arenas where legitimacy and hegemony battle for historical supremacy."[6] James Loewen reflected this perhaps most famously in 1995 with the release of his now acclaimed book *Lies My Teacher Told Me*, in which he tackled the fallacies of the Columbus and Thanksgiving stories.

Most tellingly, in a 2015 study, scholars examined the state standards for teaching Indigenous history and culture in all fifty states and found a wide variance between them. Some states include Indigenous curriculum content and some do not, but the report concluded that, overall, "Standards overwhelmingly present Indigenous Peoples in a pre-1900 context and relegate the importance and presence of Indigenous Peoples to the distant past."[7] In other words, Indians are largely portrayed as extinct.

Research on Indigenous invisibility and erasure is naturally most prevalent in Native studies, but it intersects with broader research on race and ethnicity too. Critical race theorists and sociologists point out that US society operates on a system of privilege. Systems of privilege can inhere in families, workplaces, and society in general, and are organized around the principles of domination, identification, and centeredness.[8] Whiteness is centered by default, for example: because white people tend to occupy positions of power, they possess a form of unearned privilege. Scholars emphasize the idea that racism is more than acts of individual meanness. It is built into society and functions systemically, rendering it nearly invisible. White privilege, then, stems in large part from race as a social construction. In other words, society and its state are based on a racial hierarchy in which those identified as white have always been at the top.[9] A conservative backlash after the civil rights gains of the 1960s and 1970s resulted in a widespread social denial that racism still exists. Overtly racist laws were abolished, but race and racism are still very difficult for white people to talk about.[10]

The myths about Native peoples outlined in this book grow from the racialized social structures upon which the United States is built. Because these structures are systemic, the myths tenaciously persist despite changes in law and policy over time. Ultimately they serve the settler state and by extension its international allies, who largely fail to recognize the political existence of Indigenous peoples. In the effort to dismantle the myths, the chapters that follow attempt to unpack various tenets of settler colonialism and at the same time construct a counter-narrative, one based on truth.

"ALL THE REAL INDIANS DIED OFF"

*When they got off the boat they didn't recognize us. They said
"who are you?" and we said "we're the people, the human beings."
"Oh, Indians," [they said], because they didn't recognize what it
meant to be a human being . . . but the predatory mentality shows
up and starts calling us Indians and committing genocide against
us as the vehicle of erasing the memory of being a human being.*

—John Trudell, in *Reel Injuns*

When the first Europeans came to the shores of what is now the
United States—what many descendants of the original inhabitants know as Turtle Island—they encountered enigmatic people
who challenged everything the newcomers believed about themselves and the world. The Indigenous people looked different
from them and spoke different languages, and their customs
were mysterious and frightening. They inhabited a landscape
that was entirely foreign and "wild." Perhaps most disturbing,
they were not Christians. But they had one thing the immigrants
wanted: land and the life it could give them. In the subsequent
five centuries since those early encounters, gaining access to
that land has been the central factor that has shaped the relationships between Indigenous peoples and immigrant. Those
relationships have never ceased to be vexed and conflict-ridden.
They have been and continue to be characterized by seemingly
endless ignorance, arrogance, and misunderstanding.

Where do the myths about Native people come from? What
are the motives behind them and what purpose do they serve?

To answer these questions we need to look at the ways experts in the social sciences talk about history, the nature of the society we live in, and how modern countries are formed. There is not unanimous agreement on everything, but there are certain generalities that can reasonably be claimed. For instance, some social scientists talk about the "master narratives" of a country that describe things like its national character and history. The narratives have many purposes, one of them being to construct a sense of national—or, more to the point, state—identity.[1] In countries like the United States, where citizens otherwise have very little in common with each other besides a shared language or a history of immigration, the narratives reinforce a contrived sense of unity. They reflect what acclaimed international relations scholar Benedict Anderson famously called an "imagined community."[2]

From where do the master narratives come? They are woven into the fabric of society from the start in its founding documents (like the Declaration of Independence or the US Constitution), and then gain hold through the printed word, through the mass media, through the education system. They are amplified during times of national crisis and manifested through patriotic public displays during national holidays and through the singing of national anthems at sporting events and other public gatherings. As Anderson suggested, the effervescence generated in these public spaces is itself the outward expression of this imagined unity.

A country's master narratives are not necessarily based in fact or truth. They are sometimes deliberately fictitious or contradictory of documented history. One of their purposes is to provide rationalization or justification for injustices committed against others in the name of democracy and liberty. In this way many master narratives are more like state mythologies, designed to undergird the patriotism and emotional commitment necessary in a loyal citizenry. All of the myths about American Indians emerge out of larger narratives that construct the United States as a place of exceptional righteousness, democracy, and divine guidance (manifest destiny), or what has been called "American exceptionalism." The myths tell more about the non-Native mind than they tell about Native peoples. They are clues that point to the motivations, aspirations, and ambivalence about US history and the collective identity of its citizens. We'll explore this more throughout this book.

No myth about Native people is as pervasive, pernicious, or self-serving as the myth of the vanishing Native, also known as "the vanishing Indian" or "the vanishing race." The myth, which had been building for centuries, reached an extreme at the end of the nineteenth century and the beginning of the twentieth century, a time when the Indian wars of resistance had come to a conclusion, punctuated by the massacre at Wounded Knee in 1890. In 1900 the US census counted approximately a quarter of a million Indians, a small fraction of the Indigenous population in 1492 (even based on a modest population estimate of ten million), and census figures such as this have been used to "prove" the vanishing Indian myth. It's true enough that the Native population had diminished dramatically throughout the centuries due to slavery, disease, war, and Christianization, which often took away people's names, languages, and even their clothing and hair. But the larger point to understand about the self-serving function of the myth is how it was used to advance dubious—even nefarious—political agendas aimed at the continual seizure of Indian lands and resources. It was used by both the "friends" and foes of Indians to justify policies of forced assimilation, which would mean the final solution to the "Indian problem," the ultimate disappearance of Indians to facilitate the transfer of Indian treaty lands into settler ownership.

One reason the myth of the vanishing Native has been so
pervasive is that it has been woven into history books by predominantly non-Native historians and researchers who have
wittingly or unwittingly served political agendas. But there has
been a marked shift in the way history is being told, thanks to
the increasing scholarship of Native peoples and their allies
who in the past forty to fifty years have been reframing conventional historical narratives. This reframing is often referred to
generally as postcolonial theory (or postcolonial studies), and
it views history from a larger perspective that, among other
things, recognizes the role of imperial and state power—and its
abuse—in the shaping of the modern world. It sees history in
terms of post-Columbus European and US expansionism and
the effects it had (and continues to have) on Indigenous people.
It also encompasses Native perspectives by incorporating the
growing academic field of Native American and international
Indigenous studies. This recent scholarship, sometimes deri-
sively called "revisionist history," has rendered incomplete (if
not obsolete) much of the earlier scholarship.

Within postcolonial studies is a theoretical framework
known as "settler colonialism." Viewing history through a lens
of settler colonialism entails making distinctions between the
ways colonization played out in different places, and it does
this in two fundamental ways. First, when European empires
(predominantly the English, Spanish, Dutch, Portuguese, and
French) spread into Africa and Asia, they did so primarily to
exploit natural resources such as gold, silver, other minerals,
and timber.[3] They established colonies as bases from which
to run their business enterprises and sometimes, especially
in the cases of the Spanish and the French, married into Indigenous cultures to secure better access to those resources.
For the most part, however, they didn't send large populations from the metropoles (countries or empires of origin)

into the colonies to live. Thus, in the African and Asian colonial contexts, the Indigenous peoples remained the majority populations, even though they had become dominated through military power and religious conversion. This is why the decolonization movements in those continents during the mid-twentieth century were able to reestablish Indigenous control (however problematically in, for example, Africa) and expel the foreign powers. But in the Americas, and in a few other places, like Australia and New Zealand, the colonial powers engaged in wholesale population transfer, sending massive numbers of settlers to occupy the lands (resulting in new countries after successful rebellions separated colony from the empire). And they kept coming. As these settlers came to outnumber the Indigenous populations, it became impossible for the Indigenous people to expel the invaders.

The theory of settler colonialism has gained wide acceptance among Indigenous scholars in the United States and other settler states over the last decade. It postulates, as the Australian scholar Patrick Wolfe has written, that the singular goal of the settler state relative to Indigenous peoples is the elimination of the Native in order to gain access to land.[4] The elimination of the Native can take place in a multitude of ways, including full-scale genocidal war, but it is usually more insidious than that. Not so much an overtly historical event, it becomes woven into the structure of settler society through practices that chip away at the very concept of "Native." Examples of these practices include officially encouraged intermarriage, privatization of Indigenous lands, forced assimilation via social systems like boarding schools and other educational institutions and public schools in general, citizenship bestowal, child abduction and adoption, and religious conversion, to name just a few.[5]

The myth of the vanishing Native can be traced precisely to the impulse of the state to eliminate the Native. It can be thought of as the central organizing myth from which most other popular myths about Native people arise. As the predominant myth, it is informed by the past and reaches into the present and future to continue challenging ideas about who American Indians are on a cultural level, which has ramifications at the legal level in determination of who is an Indian and who is not. It is a fully exclusionary project that limits "Native" as a category of racial and political identity. This is why deconstructing myths about American Indians is so important. At their core, the debates about Indianness are debates about authenticity. Authenticity is predicated upon specific dynamics that define "real" Indians. These are "commonsense" understandings that are built into society's dominant narratives, where certain assumptions are held to be unquestionably true. For example, real Indians are expected to look a certain way based on an appropriate minimum "blood quantum." Or real Indians live on reservations, not in cities, *and* they embody the requisite appropriate blood quantum. These examples imply an impossible ideal about Indians as frozen in an unchanging past, where they are unable to be both modern and Indian.

Today's Native studies scholarship tackles these deeply embedded stereotypes. In one study, Jeani O'Brien sought to understand how Indians were written out of New England history between 1820 and 1880, despite the fact that they continued to live in the region. Based on reading hundreds of local histories, she discovered a pattern in which Indians were not recognized as Indians (in part to justify the seizure of their lands) due to their intermarriage with non-Natives or because they lived as modern non-Native people did. O'Brien writes,

> This penchant for Indian purity as authenticity also found
> essential expression in the idea of the ancient: non-Indians
> refused to regard culture change as normative for Indian

peoples. Thus, while Indians adapted to the changes wrought by colonialism by selectively embracing new ways and ideas, such transformations stretched beyond the imaginations of New Englanders: Indians could only be ancients, and refusal to behave as such rendered Indians inauthentic in their minds.[6]

O'Brien's work—as that of numerous other scholars—is to challenge the myths that equate blood purity and cultural stasis with Native authenticity. The myth of the vanishing Indian is entirely untrue, if for no other reason than because there are currently 567 federally recognized Native nations in the United States today and because, according to the 2010 US census, 5.2 million people identified as Native American or Alaska Native, either alone or in combination with other races. About 2.9 million people identified as Native American or Alaska Native alone. But because the vanishing Indian myth is today more concerned with the authenticity of those who claim to be Indians, a nuanced argument is required, one that we will return to repeatedly. What this book is ultimately about is how society's hidden assumptions have led to the myths that persist, with mostly harmful consequences to Native people.

"Indians Were the First Immigrants to the Western Hemisphere"

In July 2012, Native journalist Simon Moya-Smith wrote with tongue in cheek about his elation at hearing Harvard professor David Reich admit that the Bering Strait land bridge story is just a theory, not a certain fact.[1] In short, Reich participated in a genetic research study that proposed that some Native Americans could be descendants of Han Chinese. When Moya-Smith interviewed Reich about the study, his most pressing concern was the Bering Strait hypothesis. Moya-Smith asked, "We all know the Bering Strait theory as just that—a theory. When did people . . . when did scientists elevate it to fact? Is it a fact?" "No," Reich replied. "I don't think it is considered fact. I think that it's a hypothesis about history, but no, it's not fact."

We can think of the land bridge theory as a master narrative that for a couple of centuries has served multiple ideological agendas, lasting despite decades of growing evidence that casts doubt on the way the story has been perpetuated in textbooks and popular media. Consider, for instance, Heather Pringle's "The First Americans," an article published in *Scientific American* in 2011.[2] Pringle documented new finds at an archaeological site at Buttermilk Creek, near Austin, Texas, revealing that humans have been present on the North American continent since at least 15,500 years ago. Her article depicts a scenario that puts people on the continent at least two thousand years earlier than previously thought—an astonishing new idea for some scientists. It details what the archaeological finds mean for scientific theories that seek to explain the "peopling" of the Americas and troubles previously held beliefs about when and how people first appeared in North America.

Pringle's thinking reflects conventional scientific theory, which postulates that the Americas were devoid of human habitation until twelve thousand or thirteen thousand years ago. As the story goes, humans originated in Africa and gradually migrated across the globe, populating places as weather, climate conditions, and the development of technology permitted. The Americas were the last vast expanse of land to see the arrival of people because of its relative isolation. Then, somewhere around seventeen thousand years ago, the last ice age locked up so much of the earth's water in ice that it caused sea levels to drop, exposing a massive section of land in the Bering Sea, creating what is referred to as the Bering Strait Land Bridge or Beringia. It was only because of the land bridge that people could eventually migrate from east to west and spread southward as the earth gradually warmed and ice sheets retreated, opening up passable routes. Some researchers believe that a small group of people—perhaps only about seventy—made the trek as the original settlers.[3] Genetic studies during the past two decades have rendered clues that connect modern-day Native Americans with Asians, providing further evidence for the theory that today's Indians are no more than yesterday's Asians.

There are also variations in the land bridge story and alternative stories explaining how people arrived in the Americas. One genetic study which produced a theory referred to as the Beringian Standstill proposes that rather than a migration that occurred fairly rapidly and with a handful of immigrants, there was a period of fifteen thousand years (give or take a few thousand years) when people camped in Beringia, effectively creating a model that argues for a three-stage migration process. In this model, humans (sometimes referred to in terms such as "Amerind Founders" and "Proto-Amerinds") gradually began traveling forty thousand years ago from East Asia into Beringia, where they paused for ten thousand years or more, eventually resuming their journey westward around sixteen thousand years ago with a "massive rush" of upwards of five thousand people.[4] The Beringian Standstill would account for the genetic mutations noted by geneticists that separate Asians and modern-day Native Americans—except, as one *National Geographic* article pointed out, there is no archaeological evidence to support it.[5] Another theory has the migration proceeding in small reed boats, traversing a coastal route from East Asia along the coast of southern Beringia and the west coast of North America.

The *Scientific American* article is notable for reasons other than its news of the archaeological find and its implications for altering the peopling time line, not the least of which are the underlying popular beliefs it evokes. Those beliefs reveal conflicts inherent in conventional science. Acclaimed Lakota scholar Vine Deloria Jr. tackled this issue nearly two decades ago in his classic book *Red Earth, White Lies: Native Americans and the Myth of Scientific Fact*. The problem, Deloria contended, is that science has become venerated as the purveyor of ultimate truth, in the way religion was before the Enlightenment. He went so far as to say that "science is simply a secular but very powerful religion."[6] Authority is all too often vested in whatever scientific theory is popular at any given moment, and "science" is often aided by the power of academic politics, sometimes even regardless of a concept's verifiability. In time, ideas that are simply theories are assumed to be the indisputable truth.

The problem about the land bridge theory for American Indians is that it contradicts their own origin stories that have been handed down orally for hundreds and even thousands of years. Science is too often ready to discredit or preclude other ways of knowing reality. Deloria wrote:

> With the triumph of Darwinian evolution as the accepted explanation of the origin of our Earth—indeed of the whole universe—we are the first society to accept a purely mechanistic origin for ourselves and the teeming life we find on planet Earth. Science tells us that this whole panorama of life, our deepest experiences, and our most cherished ideas and emotions are really just the result of a fortunate combination of amino acids happening to coalesce billions of years ago and that our most profound experiences are simply electrical impulses derived from the logical consequence of that action. . . . Inconsistencies abound, but we are so brainwashed by science that we do not even ask the relatively simple questions about ordinary things.[7]

An example is the Bering Strait theory: Deloria devoted an entire chapter to rejecting it, based on what he saw as irreconcilable facts in the research that led to its creation, and the suppression of research that doesn't support the theory.

It is interesting to note that at least one science writer, Annalee Newitz, has characterized the Buttermilk Creek find as "a major blow against the Bering Strait theory of migration."[8] In 2014 another archaeological find, this one in Brazil, pointed to a similar conclusion. Stone tools unearthed at Serra da Capivara National Park in northeastern Brazil places humans in the area at least twenty-two thousand years ago. According to a *New York Times* article:

> [The] discovery adds to the growing body of research upending a prevailing belief of 20th-century archaeology in the United States known as the Clovis model, which holds that

people first arrived in the Americas from Asia about 13,000 years ago. "If they're right, and there's a great possibility that they are, that will change everything we know about the settlement of the Americas," said Walter Neves, an evolutionary anthropologist at the University of São Paulo whose own analysis of an 11,000-year-old skull in Brazil implies that some ancient Americans resembled aboriginal Australians more than they did Asians.[9]

Also in 2014, Native American science writer Alex Ewen wrote an ambitious six-part series for Indian Country Today Media Network debunking the Bering Strait theory.[10] In the series, Ewen traces the history of the theory to a time when science was subject to—and a subset of—Christian theology. Based on biblical scripture, because humans couldn't have been on the planet more than a few thousand years, they couldn't have been in the Americas for more than five thousand years, and scientists bent their theories accordingly. Theories that constructed Indigenous peoples as genetically inferior to white Europeans (what has become known as "scientific racism," explored in more detail in myth 7) competed with ideas about Indians as genetic descendants of Europeans or even the supposed Lost Tribe of Israel, leading eventually to the land bridge theory. But then in the nineteenth century as the fields of paleoanthropology and archaeology evolved and began acknowledging human antiquity far beyond a few thousand years, they too were subjected to ideological tyranny—this time, however, coming from previous generations of scientists who were unwilling to accept new evidence that would challenge their ideas about a singular human migration over a hypothetical land bridge within the previous five thousand years. Among the milestone evidentiary finds were the 1927 and 1932 discoveries of spear points near Clovis, New Mexico (now referred to as the "Clovis First" theory), that dated human presence in North America to at least ten thousand years previous, pushing back the land bridge time line by thousands of years. In another significant archaeological discovery, in 1949 human campsites found in Lewisville, Texas, were radiocarbon-dated thirty-seven thousand years old, but the findings were stubbornly resisted for decades. Then, in the mid-1980s, the radiocarbon dating technique itself was shown to be problematic when it was discovered that post–Cold War atomic bomb testing added carbon 14 to the environment, pushing dates (such as the Clovis finds) back as much as two thousand years, delivering another blow to the land bridge theory.

The scientific milestones throughout the nineteenth and twentieth centuries chronicled by Ewen have eroded the land bridge hypothesis despite scientists' stubborn adherence to rigid ideologies. More recent biological and linguistic studies have pointed to evidence of ancient seafaring and two-way migrations, casting a growing shadow on the land bridge single-migration narrative. The rigid adherence to ideology in the face of new information amounts to the politicization of science and is the underlying dynamic upon which so much science and science writing about Native peoples—and the *Scientific American* article in particular—is based.

The politicization of science—especially relative to the land bridge theory—would reach new heights (or lows, as the case may be) with the discovery of the so-called Kennewick Man. In 1996, a nearly complete skeleton was discovered in the shallows of the Columbia River on federally owned land near Kennewick in Washington State, in the vicinity of historical homelands of several extant Indian nations. Early anatomically based assessments indicated that the skeleton was not Native American, which, if proven, would enable the bones to be turned over to scientists for extensive study. The skeleton was determined to be a man between forty and fifty-five years old and his bones radiocarbon-dated to approximately nine thousand years before present.[11] At first scientists speculated that he was Caucasian, which bolstered their arguments that Kennewick Man be handed over to them. Later, based on measurements of his skull, he was thought to be of Polynesian or possibly Japanese Ainu origin. The early assessments also determined that Kennewick Man (called by local Indians "the Ancient One"), rather mysteriously, lived on a diet of marine animals and water from glacial melt. DNA technology, however, was not advanced enough at the time to determine his genetic connections. If it were true that the Ancient One was not genetically related to Indigenous North Americans, this would present powerful new evidence for the multiple migrations idea, punching bigger holes in the conventional single-migration Bering Strait narrative.

After the preliminary tests led to the conclusion that the skeleton was ancient, the US Army Corps of Engineers (under whose jurisdiction the skeleton fell) prepared to turn the remains over to local Native nations to be reburied under the Native American Graves Protection and Repatriation Act (NAGPRA).[12] But a small group of individual scientists, believing that since the skeleton was likely not Native American and should be kept available for scientific analysis, sued the federal government to obtain the remains for study. After several years of contentious litigation, in 2004 the final ruling of a federal appellate court was that Kennewick Man was not Indian and therefore not subject to NAGPRA.

Nearly ten years after the Ancient One was discovered, the bones were turned over by the Army Corps for study over a total of sixteen days, and this study was conducted in July 2005 and February 2006.[13] In 2014 the results were published in an exhaustive 680-page book, *Kennewick Man: The Scientific Investigation of an Ancient American Skeleton*, edited by Douglas Owsley and Richard Jantz.[14] The book concludes that Kennewick Man was a traveler from the far north. All seemed settled until June 2015, when, in a predictable twist of fate (predictable at least to Indians), the results of DNA testing done in Denmark revealed that the Ancient One was more genetically related to the Colville Indians—one of the Native communities in the region where he was found—than anyone else in the modern world. It remains to be seen what will happen next, but more court battling to have the bones repatriated as per NAGPRA seems inevitable.

The Kennewick Man saga was a painful reminder to American Indians that, even in the twenty-first century, science is not above politics, and the power to define who Native people are—and thus who their ancestors were—is always political. As Bruce Elliot Johansen argues, in his book *Native Peoples of North America*, archaeology is shaped by racial politics.[15] Scientists had constructed racialized images of Kennewick Man based on very scant evidence—at first a Caucasian Patrick Stewart looka-like, and then an imaginary ancient Ainu—that ultimately suited scientists' own needs and ignored not only the Indians' beliefs but their rights too.

The Bering Strait theory is an increasingly slippery slope that can at best be thought of as only one among numerous possible scenarios for the peopling of the Americas. Even the National Park Service acknowledges the uncertainty on its website:

In today's world, the peopling of the Americas is a hotly debated topic. Evidence for competing theories continues to change the ways we understand our prehistoric roots. As of 2008, genetic findings are suggesting that a single population of modern humans migrated from southern Siberia toward the land mass known as the Bering Land Bridge as early as 30,000 years ago, and crossed over to the Americas by 16,500 years ago. Archaeological evidence shows that by 15,000 years ago, humans had made it south of the Canadian ice sheets.

While this may represent the earliest migration, it was not the only one. Once the first humans made it over, it appears that multiple migrations took place over the next several millennia, not only across the ice-free corridor, but also along the coast by boat.

Evidence is still sparse and often conflicting however, so theories of the "first Americans" are still largely inconclusive.[16] [Emphasis added]

"COLUMBUS DISCOVERED AMERICA"

Old myths die hard, it is said, and few die harder than the Columbus discovery myth. The claim that Columbus discovered America is the original prevarication that laid the foundation for a national mythology at whose center is the deliberate discursive erasure of Indigenous peoples. The statement itself is a misnomer. "America" as it is usually understood refers to the United States of America, but most people understand that in 1492 the United States was still 284 years into the future. The use of the term "America" as a synonym for "United States" also ignores the rest of North America, as well as Central and South America, where countless others refer to themselves as "Americans" (Latin Americans), so the term is far too broad to have any real meaning beyond reference to the Western Hemisphere. If we are to be accurate about a national origin myth of discovery, it would be more appropriate to say that Columbus discovered the Bahamas, Hispaniola, and Cuba.

Except that from an Indigenous viewpoint, he didn't actually discover anything. Indigenous peoples assert instead (not necessarily humorously) that they discovered Columbus. Not only could Columbus not have discovered a country that didn't yet exist—or play any actual role in its creation—but he also utterly failed to comprehend, let alone respect, the people he stumbled upon in the mistaken belief that he had arrived in the "East Indies." He wasn't the first European to sail to the Americas anyway, and he never even set foot on the continent we know today as North America during any of his four journeys.[1] He did, however, set into motion a tidal wave of destruction so cataclysmic that many scholars believe it is unparalleled in recorded history. From an Indigenous standpoint, he has been wrongfully venerated. He is widely credited with initiating the transatlantic slave trade and catalyzing a genocide from which Native people are still recovering. The Columbus discovery story can be thought of as the greatest piece of propaganda of the last five centuries.

A growing abundance of scholarship and popular literature in the past few decades has deconstructed the actual history of Cristóbal Colón's odyssey to the "New World," unraveling the singular portrayal of Columbus as a hero, much to the chagrin of some conventional scholars. Columbus's stalwart apologists—while sometimes acknowledging the atrocities and the flaws of the man—nonetheless continue to view history through a lens that presumes the inevitability of modernity (i.e., European superiority) and use the celebratory term "Age of Exploration" for Columbus's times.[2]

Beginning in colonial times, Columbus was widely lionized as a national hero. In 1906 Colorado became the first state to establish an official holiday in his honor, and in 1937 Columbus Day gained federal status. Then Samuel Eliot Morison penned the two-volume *Admiral of the Ocean Sea*, based on his own ambitious re-creation of Columbus's first voyage in a three-masted ship. The book won the Pulitzer Prize for literature in 1943 and earned Morison a reputation as the preeminent scholar on Columbus in the United States. A naval admiral and quintessential American patriot, Morison praised Columbus for "his indomitable will, his superb faith in God and in his own mission as the Christ-bearer to lands beyond the sea."

With the rise of ethnic studies in the post–civil rights era, scholars began shining light on the darker parts of the Columbus story, particularly in publications such as Howard Zinn's

A People's History of the United States (1980), Kirkpatrick Sale's *Christopher Columbus and the Conquest of Paradise* (1990), David Stannard's *American Holocaust* (1992), Jan Carew's *The Rape of Paradise: Columbus and the Birth of Racism in the Americas* (1994), and James Loewen's *Lies My Teacher Told Me* (1995). These and other authors drew from primary and secondary sources to reassess Columbus's legacy, painting a more honest—if disturbing—picture of the historical reality and its consequences. For European settler descendants they may be inconvenient truths, but for the Indigenous peoples of the Americas, with millennia-long memories, Columbus's arrival is a devastating recent occurrence still viscerally felt. Without attempting to recount all the documentary evidence that exposes Columbus's inhumanity and the fallout of his intrusions, we'll highlight those most relevant to Indigenous peoples, most of which derive directly from Columbus's own logs and other eyewitness accounts, primarily the priest Bartolomé de Las Casas.

COLUMBUS CAPTURED AND ENSLAVED INDIGENOUS PEOPLES

By the time Columbus made his first journey across the Atlantic, he'd been a slave trader for twelve years under the Portuguese flag, but initially it was gold he was looking for, not slaves.[3] He first made landfall in the Bahamas, where he was greeted by friendly Arawaks who gave Columbus and his men food, water, and gifts. He noticed that they wore small bits of gold jewelry, which would have tragic consequences for the Arawaks. Columbus wrote in his log:

> They . . . brought us parrots and balls of cotton and spears and many other things, which they exchanged for the glass beads and hawks' bells. They willingly traded everything they owned. . . . They were well-built, with good bodies and handsome features. . . . They do not bear arms, and do not

know them, for I showed them a sword, they took it by the
edge and cut themselves out of ignorance. They have no iron.
Their spears are made of cane. . . . They would make fine servants. . . . With fifty men we could subjugate them all and make
them do whatever we want.[4]

"As soon as I arrived in the Indies," Columbus would later
write, "on the first Island which I found, I took some of the natives by force in order that they might learn and might give me
information of whatever there is in these parts."[5]

It was gold Columbus wanted to know about, and as soon as
he made landfall he began terrorizing the Indigenous people,
taking captives, including women as sex slaves for the men. On
his first voyage he took between ten and twenty-five captives
back to Europe, seven or eight of whom survived the voyage. By
the second voyage, which was outfitted with seventeen heavily
armed ships, attack dogs, and more than twelve hundred men,
the mission was to acquire not just gold but slaves. During that
expedition, fifteen hundred men, women, and children were
captured, with five hundred sent back to Europe on ships, two
hundred dying on the way.[6] According to Loewen, Columbus
is thought to have enslaved five thousand Indigenous peoples
throughout his voyaging career to the Americas, more than enslaved by any other individual ever.

COLUMBUS INSTIGATED THE GENOCIDE OF INDIGENOUS AMERICANS

The small gold ornaments worn by the Arawaks triggered a
bloodlust so extreme that the historical record, while clear,
is difficult to comprehend. To read the primary sources and
still keep in mind Columbus as hero creates cognitive disso-
nance. On his first journey, Columbus set up a base on the island of Hispaniola (today's Dominican Republic and Haiti) that
he named Fort Navidad. Bartolomé de Las Casas's father and

uncles journeyed with Columbus on his second voyage and afterward became wealthy from sharing in the Spanish plunder of Hispaniola, and Bartolomé came to the Americas in 1502 to see the family's holdings. In a three-volume work titled *Historia de las Indias* (*History of the Indies*), which covered the years up to 1520, Las Casas recorded in excruciating detail the fate of the Indigenous peoples, from what he witnessed firsthand. Imagining huge fields of gold, which did not exist, Columbus instituted what later became known as the *encomienda* system, large estates run on forced labor for the purposes of extracting gold. Las Casas reported that when mining quotas were not met by the Indians excavating the gold, their hands were cut off and they bled to death. When they attempted to flee, they were hunted down with dogs and killed. So little gold existed in Hispaniola that the island turned into a massive killing field. The Arawaks eventually took to mass suicide and infanticide to escape the cruelty of the Spaniards. "In two years," Howard Zinn wrote, "through murder, mutilation, or suicide, half of the 250,000 Indians on Haiti were dead. . . . By the year 1515, there were perhaps fifty thousand Indians left. By 1550, there were five hundred. A report of the year 1650 shows none of the original Arawaks or their descendants left on the island."[7]

Indigenous peoples perished by the millions in the first century of European contact throughout the Caribbean and the rest of the Americas, from diseases brought by the Europeans, all stemming from Columbus's initial voyage. In many cases entire nations were extinguished. Indigenous population density in pre-contact North and South America has been a hotly debated topic among scholars for decades. Alfred Kroeber estimated the number at an extremely conservative 8.4 million, Henry Dobyns put it at 100 million, while Cherokee anthropologist Russell Thornton, known for his study of Native American population history, believes that 75 million is more realistic.[8]

Kroeber estimated 900,000 in North America on the low end, Dobyns believed it was 18 million north of Mesoamerica, while Thornton advanced a more moderate figure of "7+ million."[9] By 1890, 228,000 American Indians were counted in the United States, a time scholars generally agree was the nadir of the Indigenous population in the country. If we use Thornton's number, seven million, 228,000 represents a population decline of roughly 97 percent. As Thornton notes, however, the population decline cannot be attributed merely to disease: "Native American populations were probably reduced not only by the direct and indirect effects of disease but also by direct and indirect effects of wars and genocide, enslavement, removals and relocations, and changes in American Indian societies, cultures, and subsistence patterns accompanying European colonialism."[10]

In other words, American Indians today can be said to have survived genocide of apocalyptic proportions, more dramatic than any other in recorded history.

COLUMBUS'S VOYAGES LED TO THE DOCTRINE OF DISCOVERY

Aside from the enduring legacy of genocide and slavery, for American Indians and other Indigenous peoples in the Americas and elsewhere Columbus's influence is felt today in the doctrine of discovery. The doctrine is a legal principle based on the underlying philosophy that the European "discovery" of the Americas confers a superior form of title to land. The doctrine has its roots in the Roman Catholic Church and is a tenet of international law that traces its origins to the Crusades in the Holy Land between the eleventh and thirteenth centuries.[11] Based on the universal authority of the pope, who was considered to be "vested with a supreme spiritual jurisdiction over the souls of all humankind," the Catholic Church essentially declared war on all "pagans," "heathens," and "infidels" until they submitted by converting to Christianity and distributed their lands

among the European Christian monarchs.[12] The order and justification for these aggressions were codified in edicts issued by
the papacy, called "papal bulls," and were legally binding. Well
before Columbus's voyages, the first papal bull granting European dominion beyond Europe can be traced to Pope Nicholas
V's issue of the bull Dum Diversas in 1452, which authorized
Portugal to reduce Muslims, pagans, and other nonbelievers
to perpetual slavery and to seize their property, and which fa-
cilitated the Portuguese slave trade from West Africa.[13] In 1454
the bull known as Romanus Pontifex granted a monopoly on
the African slave trade to Portugal and reinforced the European
imperative to subdue all non-Christians by enslavement and
land seizure.[14] After Columbus's first voyage, Pope Alexander
VI issued the notorious bull Inter Caetera in 1493, granting the
newly "discovered" lands to Spain.[15] Altogether the papal bulls
Dum Diversas, Romanus Pontifex of 1454, and Inter Ceatera
"came to serve as the basis and justification for the Doctrine
of Discovery, the global slave-trade of the 15th and 16th centuries, and the Age of Imperialism."[16]

Centuries later, US jurists (including US Supreme Court chief
justice John Marshall) would refer to this history in their articulations of an emerging body of federal Indian law. In the first of
such articulations, in *Johnson v. M'Intosh* (1823), Marshall argued
that "the superior genius of Europe" claimed an ascendancy over
the Indigenous peoples and that the bestowal of civilization and
Christianity was ample compensation to the inhabitants. "The
law [governing] the right of acquisition," he wrote, said that
"discovery gave title to the government by whose subjects, or by
whose authority, it was made, against all other European governments, which title might be consummated by possession."[17]

The doctrine of discovery is to this day one of the bedrock
principles by which the United States administers its relationship with American Indians. Indigenous inferiority and

European superiority is thus still affirmed as the predominant paradigm in federal Indian law. For legal scholar Robert A. Williams Jr., the doctrine of discovery is part of a language of racism that has guided the US Supreme Court since *Johnson v. M'Intosh*. It finds its way into modern court decisions, as if *Plessy v. Ferguson* were still being used as a basis for African American civil rights.[18] Native American scholars David E. Wilkins and K. Tsianina Lomawaima contend that the doctrine has competing interpretations that have worked to preclude Indians' rights to own their own lands. They argue for a "preemptive" interpretation, in which discovery means that "discovering" nations were granted merely "an exclusive, preemptive right to purchase Indian land, if the tribe agreed to sell any of its territory," a right in view of competing European powers, not an interpretation construed as conquest.[19] The discovery doctrine is such a complex topic that we discuss other aspects of it further in myth 6.

Columbus Day was once widely celebrated all over the Western Hemisphere. Since the 1990s, with the growing awareness in the United States of the dark legacy associated with Columbus, there has been a growing movement to abolish Columbus Day and to instead recognize the survival of Indigenous peoples. Perhaps the earliest effort in the United States came with the formation of the Transform Columbus Day Alliance in Denver in 1989, which still exists as a coalition of over eighty organizations who oppose the city's Columbus Day celebration and parade. Most visible of those organizations is the American Indian Movement (AIM). Every year some Denver residents and AIM members face off in heated confrontations when American Indians protest against the parade, with particularly vitriolic responses from those Italian Americans who view the protests as anti-Italian.[20]

People in other cities and governments have had far more success in their campaigns to abolish Columbus Day. Berkeley, for example, was the first city to officially change Columbus Day to Indigenous Peoples Day in 1992, the year of the Columbus quincentennial. Preceding Berkeley, in 1990 South Dakota renamed Columbus Day Native American Day. Hawaii in 1988 enacted Discovers' Day, the second Monday of October, "in recognition of the Polynesian discoverers of the Hawaiian islands, provided that this day is not and shall not be construed to be a state holiday."[21] And since 2014 a snowball effect has seen quite a number of other places relinquish Columbus Day for Indigenous Peoples Day, including Minneapolis; Seattle; Albuquerque; Anchorage; Anadarko, Oklahoma; Portland, Oregon; and Olympia, Washington.

The movement to jettison Columbus Day in the United States is part of a larger global movement to renounce what Indigenous peoples and other social justice activists view as a celebration of "murder, rape, slavery, torture, and genocide in our community and churches."[22] In Latin America, most countries celebrate El Día de la Raza instead of Columbus Day.[23] Argentina celebrates Día del Respecto a la Diversidad Cultural (Day of Respect for Cultural Diversity). In Buenos Aires in 2015, with great fanfare, a statue of Columbus outside the presidential palace was replaced with a fifty-two-foot-high bronze statue of Juana Azurduy, a nineteenth-century Argentine military leader of mestizo (mixed Indigenous and Spanish) heritage. Bolivian president Evo Morales attended the statue's official inauguration with Argentina's president Cristina Fernandez.

"Thanksgiving Proves the Indians Welcomed the Pilgrims"

Second only to the Columbus discovery story, the Thanksgiving tale is the United States' quintessential origin narrative. Like the Columbus myth, the story of Thanksgiving has morphed into an easily digestible narrative that, despite its actual underlying truths, is designed to reinforce a sense of collective patriotic pride. The truths are, however, quite well documented. Their concealment within a simplistic story inevitably depicts a convoluted reality about the Indigenous peoples who played crucial roles in both events, and it presents an exaggerated valorization about the settlers' roles. The result is a collective amnesia that fuels the perpetuation of Native American stereotypes, playing out over and over again in the classrooms and textbooks of American schoolchildren, generation after generation. This only masks the complexities of the relationships between settlers and Indians, and thus the founding of the United States.

The Thanksgiving story as we know it is a story of unconditional welcome by the Indigenous peoples, a feel-good narrative that rationalizes and justifies the uninvited settlement of a foreign people by painting a picture of an organic friendship. A more accurate telling of the story, however, describes the forming of political alliances built on a mutual need for survival and an Indigenous struggle for power in the vacuum left by a destructive century of foreign settlement.

THE BACKSTORY

The offenses of the Thanksgiving story stem from lack of historical context. For example, it often gives the impression that the *Mayflower* pilgrims were the first Europeans to settle on the land today known as the United States. But by the time the *Mayflower* arrived at Plymouth, Massachusetts, in December 1620, Europeans had been traveling to the North American continent, and founding colonies there, for well over a century. Armed with information about the region—made available by the knowledge and mapping of predecessors like Samuel de Champlain—the Eastern Seaboard was dotted with numerous European enclaves and towns. Jamestown, for example, was founded in 1607, while Florida had been populated by the Spanish since the founding of St. Augustine, in 1565. Some colonies, such as the one in Roanoke, Virginia, had failed. The *Mayflower* immigrants, who came to be known as the Pilgrims, were thus, in December 1620, only the latest newcomers to the land, all of which was known at the time to the English as Virginia. Exposure to European diseases had resulted in pandemics among the Natives up and down the coast from Florida to New England throughout the sixteenth century, exacerbated by the Indian slave trade started by Columbus. Between 1616 and 1619 the region that would soon become Plymouth Colony underwent an unknown epidemic that decimated the Indigenous population by at least one third to as much as 90 percent—a fact the Pilgrims knew and exploited.[1]

The settlement the Pilgrims called New Plymouth was the ancestral land of the Wampanoag (Pokanoket) people, who called the place Patuxet. Contrary to the popular myth that the Pilgrims arrived to an unoccupied "wilderness," it had for untold generations been a well-managed landscape, cleared and maintained for cornfields and crops like beans and squash, as well as for game. Also contrary to popular mythology, the

Wampanoags, like most eastern Indians, were farmers, not no-mads. Up until the epidemic, the Wampanoag nation had been large and powerful, organized into sixty-nine villages in what is today southeastern Massachusetts and eastern Rhode Island. Their exact population is unknown, but estimates range from twenty-four thousand to upwards of one hundred thousand.[2] The epidemic decimated their population, however, and desta-bilized relations with their traditional enemies, the neighbor-ing Narragansett, Mohegan, and Pequot peoples, among others. In 1620 the Wampanoags were in a state of military tension, if not full-scale war with the Narragansetts.

When the Pilgrims arrived at New Plymouth in the depth of winter, food was the first concern. From colonists' journal entries we know that right after their arrival Native homes and graves were robbed of food and other items. Written accounts describe taking "things" for which they "intended" to pay later. Ever pious and believing in divine predestination, the religious separatists attributed their good fortune to God, "for how else could we have done it without meeting some Indians who might trouble us."[3] Thus, the Pilgrims' survival that first winter can be attributed to Indians both alive and dead.

Before the epidemic, Patuxet had been a village with around two thousand people.[4] Months after their arrival, the colonists had their first serious encounter with an Indian. In March 1621 they came face to face with Samoset, a Wampanoag sachem (leader) of a confederation of about twenty villages.[5] In rudi-mentary English learned from English fisherman and trappers, Samoset explained about the plague that had just swept through the area. He also told them about Massasoit, who was considered the head Wampanoag sachem, also known as a sagamore. Within a few days, Massasoit appeared at the Plymouth colony accom-panied by Tisquantum (Squanto), eager to form an alliance with the colonists in light of the shifting balance of power in the

Indigenous world due to the plague.⁶ A formal treaty was immediately negotiated, outlining relationships of peace and mutual
protection. Massasoit sent Squanto as a liaison between the Native confederation and the colonists, and Squanto taught them
Native planting techniques that ensured the bountiful harvest
they would enjoy in the fall. Squanto had been kidnapped as a
child, sold into slavery, and sent to England, where he learned
how to speak English. Having escaped under extraordinary circumstances, he found passage back to Patuxet in 1619 only to
find himself the sole male survivor of his village.⁷

THE FIRST THANKSGIVING

The facts about the first Thanksgiving come from two primary
written sources, Edward Winslow's *Mourt's Relation* and William
Bradford's *Of Plimouth Plantation*.⁸ Neither of the accounts are
detailed enough to surmise the familiar tale of Pilgrims hosting
a feast to thank the Indians for their help, certainly not enough
to imagine Englishmen teaching the Indians about thanksgiving
as we are sometimes led to believe. The English had an ancient
custom of harvest festivals that had been secular, not religious
affairs. Spiritual ceremonials of gratitude had always been central cultural attributes among Indigenous peoples who believed
in relationships of reciprocity, so the concept of thanksgiving
was not new to either group.⁹

Only Winslow's account, written several weeks after the
event, mentions the Indians' participation. He wrote:

Our harvest being gotten in, our governor sent four men on
fowling, that so we might after a special manner rejoice together, after we had gathered the fruits of our labors; they four
in one day killed as much fowl, as with a little help beside,
served the Company almost a week, at which time amongst
other Recreations, we exercised our Arms, many of the Indians

coming amongst us, and amongst the rest their greatest king Massasoit, with some ninety men, whom for three days we entertained and feasted, and they went out and killed five Deer, which they brought to the Plantation and bestowed on our Governor, and upon the Captain and others. And although it be not always so plentiful, as it was at this time with us, yet by the goodness of God, we are so far from want, that we often wish you partakers of our plenty.[10]

Not all historians agree as to what actually happened that day. It is clear that the colonists decided to have a harvest celebration (note that nowhere is the word "thanksgiving" used). As can be deduced from the account, one widely espoused interpretation holds that the Indians were not initially invited to share in the celebration. They came when they heard in the distance the discharge of guns, fired in the exuberance of the festivities. Wondering if there was trouble, the Wampanoags entered the English village with around ninety men. It was only after arriving well-intentioned but uninvited that an invitation to stay was extended. Since there wasn't enough food to go around, the Indians went out and caught some deer, which they ceremonially presented to the English.[11]

Throughout *Mourt's Relation* (written over a period of one year from November 1620 to November of 1621) references are made to the affection and camaraderie between the Plymouth colonists and Massasoit and Squanto, but the tenuous peace was to be short-lived.[12] Acting independently, Squanto had developed rogue tendencies in an apparent power struggle with Massasoit.[13] He increasingly undermined the authority of Massasoit and other sachems, eventually driving a fatal wedge between himself and Massasoit and straining the relations between Massasoit and the colony. By the spring of 1622, Massasoit had ended trade between the confederation and the

English, and the colony held on desperately to their relationship with Squanto. In October Squanto died under mysterious conditions. Nataniel Philbrick wrote that although it is difficult to document, he may have been poisoned in an assassination plot masterminded by Massasoit.[14]

Within a few months Massasoit had reestablished diplomatic relations with the colony. He appointed Hobamok as his intermediary, and an uneasy alliance was maintained with the colony until Massasoit's death around 1661. He would be succeeded by his son Wamsutta, and by 1662 his second son, Metacom, known to the English as King Philip, was in charge. Because of the unrelenting pressure of the English demands for land, relations would deteriorate so severely between the English and the Wampanoags that by 1675, war broke out. Called King Philip's War, it has come to be seen as the bloodiest, most violent conflict ever fought on American soil. Thus, in light of the larger history, the simplistic idea that Thanksgiving proves that the Indians welcomed the Pilgrims can be more accurately seen as a temporary chapter characterized by maximized political self-interest on all sides.

"INDIANS WERE SAVAGE AND WARLIKE"

*He [King George] has excited domestic insurrections amongst us,
and has endeavored to bring on the inhabitants of our frontiers,
the merciless Indian savages, whose known rule of warfare, is
undistinguished destruction of all ages, sexes and conditions.*

—Declaration of Independence

Most US Americans are surprised to learn that Thomas Jefferson, principal author of the Declaration of Independence in 1776, penned these words. They conclude a list of grievances against Britain's King George III that rationalized the colonists' move to secede from the empire. The words contradict all that is considered sacred about the document—its theoretical commitments to equality and those "certain inalienable rights": life, liberty, and the pursuit of happiness. Indians are clearly not part of this equation as they were considered a separate people (and not quite human). The enshrinement of such pernicious language within a foundational state text presents an unreconciled ideological conundrum in a republic dedicated to democracy. It also solidifies a representation of Native people in the American imagination in a way that has yet to be fully transcended. This has manifested as ongoing justification for the profound level of violence committed against Indigenous populations over centuries of colonial invasion. It also simultaneously—if paradoxically—denies that violence.

The underlying logic is all too familiar: because Indians were by nature "savage and warlike" (violent), they needed to be

exterminated or civilized by the superior Europeans. The implication was that because Europeans were conversely less violent
(i.e., "civilized"), they were more deserving of the land (which
was divinely ordained), and thus conquest by any means was
necessary. Literature written throughout centuries of US history
and today's body of federal Indian law reflects this logic. More
recent critical scholarship, however, exposes the deeply bigoted
assumptions and inherent deceptions that drive the logic.

By the time Thomas Jefferson incorporated the words about
Indian savagery into the Declaration, the concept was already
centuries old. In reality, Europeans had made up their minds
that Indians were savages before they'd even encountered them.
According to the Online Etymology Dictionary, the word "savage" originated around the twelfth century from the French
"sauvage," which means "wild, savage, untamed, strange, pagan"
and stems from the Latin "silvaticus," meaning "of the woods."[1]
The word thus has religious connotations: non-Christian peoples, encountered and yet to be encountered, who did not live
like European Christians, were savages by default.[2] Closely related is the far older concept of "barbarian," with its roots in
the Greek, which literally referred to people who spoke a foreign
language. With the rise of the Roman Empire the term came to
be associated with people considered to be less civilized.[3] By
the sixteenth century, the terms "savage" and "barbarian" were
used interchangeably, colored as they were by religious dogma.
Even Bartolomé de Las Casas, that early defender of Indigenous
peoples, conceded that Indians were barbarians simply because
they weren't Christians.[4] In the 1580 essay "On Cannibals," the
French philosopher Michel de Montaigne pointed out, however,
that "everyone gives the title of barbarism to everything that is
not in use in his own country."[5] In more modern parlance, Europe had its own ethnocentrism. Still, by the mid-nineteenth
century, the idea of savagery and barbarism that presumed

Indigenous others to be in a natural subhuman stage of development was widely accepted as scientific fact. (Scientific racism is discussed in more detail in myth 7.)

Jefferson accused the English king of enlisting Indians in defense of the Crown's colonies against the separatists. Since the beginning of the European incursions on the North American continent, Indians had been drawn into the struggles for land and power among the colonizing empires, and this sometimes occurred within a context of ongoing conflict between the Indian nations themselves. These conditions were complicated and exacerbated by foreign-borne disease and the Indian slave trade that Europeans introduced. Nations were pitted against nations against a backdrop of the colonists' insatiable greed for land. The French and Indian War (in which most of the northeastern Indians had fought for the French) had in the previous decade ended in a costly victory for the British, culminating with the Proclamation of 1763. This imposed a limit on the expansion of British settlement, ostensibly to protect the Indians, and angered settlers. It ultimately became a contributing factor to the Revolutionary War, adding to the colonists' grievances against the king. However, Jefferson's claim that the Indians' "known rule of warfare is undistinguished destruction of all ages, sexes and conditions" was pure hyperbole that only fanned the flames of war. It might even be seen as a projection of settler innocence.[6] In truth, the Europeans practiced a far more vicious style of warfare, and comparative studies on militarism between the Indians and their Anglo counterparts bear this out.

Indigenous peoples were not pacifists, but their very different military styles reflect dramatically different reasons for fighting compared to the Europeans. Furthermore, many analyses reveal that their warfare patterns changed after the coming of the Europeans. In the Northeast the prevailing form of fighting among Native peoples took the form of what are usually referred to as mourning wars. Mourning wars were low-intensity, low-casualty conflicts mostly driven by the desire to avenge the death of a community member, be they warrior or other kin.[7] Rarely were military conflicts the kinds of large-scale, destructive affairs they had been in Europe. Military tactics centered on raiding or ambush, utilizing the element of surprise to simply kill members of an enemy group but more often to take captives. Captives typically were kept and incorporated into the community to replace lost relatives, but they could also be ritually executed in ways that strike us today as brutal forms of torture.[8] The feuds could last for generations. Based on these practices, early European chroniclers of Indian warfare (often Jesuit missionaries) notoriously depicted Indians as "bloodthirsty savages who waged war for mere sport," but, as historian Daniel Richter notes, "only in recent decades have ethnohistorians discarded such shibboleths and begun to study Indian wars in the same economic and diplomatic frameworks long used by students of European conflicts."[9] From this perspective mourning wars had three pragmatic social functions: to restore lost population, to ensure social continuity, and to provide a way for a community to process grief.[10] At their core these functions maintained spiritual and political power. With the arrival of the Europeans came trade, more disease, firearms, and new enemies, ultimately making the mourning wars, at least for a time, far deadlier and more complex than they had been.

In the Great Plains, while there is some archaeological evidence for pre-contact high casualty warfare in a few regions, low-intensity warfare was the norm.[11] In the Great Plains, Great Basin, and Southwest, raiding and captive-taking occurred for reasons similar to those behind the mourning wars, becoming far more violent with Spanish colonization and its attendant market imperatives, which would entail the transatlantic slave trade.[12] Prior to European arrival, conflict was a localized phenomenon.[13]

While Indigenous military strategies are usually described as irregular and insurgent, by contrast European-style warfare have been thought of as "regular," characterized by state-controlled standing armies and the ideology of the "just" or "honorable war," in which certain restraint was exercised.[14] Sybelle Schiepers, referencing the work of Ian Steele, points out, however, that such restraint was limited to other Europeans. "Native Americans, on the other hand," Schiepers writes, "met with far more ruthless treatment."[15] Indeed, according to John Grenier, Americans' "first way of war" combined irregular methods with unlimited objectives, creating "a military tradition that accepted, legitimized, and encouraged attacks upon and the destruction of noncombatants, villages and agricultural resources."[16] From the very earliest military conflicts between settlers and Indians, the Europeans showed the magnitude of their brutality. The Jamestown Wars on the Powhatans initiated in 1609, for example, began with threats from military leader John Smith that all the women and children would be killed if the Powhatans refused to feed, clothe, and provide land and labor to the settlers. The threats were carried out with the killing of all the Powhatan children, with the gruesome details bragged about in a report by the mercenary George Percy.[17] In the Tidewater War (1644–46), the colonists conducted a campaign of continual village and crop raids designed to starve out the Indians, and, with the Powhatans largely gone, the settlers brought in enslaved Africans and indentured European servants to do the work.[18] Best-selling author Nathaniel Philbrick contends that "with the Pequot War in 1637 New England was introduced to the horrors of European-style genocide."[19]

Arguably the biggest difference between Indian and European (and Euro-American) warfare was their rationale. As reflected by the example of the mourning wars, Indians fought essentially to maintain social or economic stability, not to control others or to expand their settlements.[20] Europeans, on the other hand, fought full-spectrum hegemonic wars in order to acquire territory, expand economies, or impose religious domination, goals that were often indistinguishable, especially in the Americas.[21] This deadly triumvirate was the very foundation of Europe's empire-building projects—at the behest of the church—that drove Spanish, English, French, Dutch, and Portuguese exploits into the Americas. And no one was going to get in their way, least of all some savage Indians.

The narrative of Indian savagery is a lie told so many times that it became "truth" in the American mind. It was one of the necessary truths used to justify European and later American violence against Indigenous peoples to fulfill the demands of imperialism—unlimited expansion at all costs. And as Ned Blackhawk contends, it is this history of violence that has been largely ignored in American historiography in order to preserve an image of all that is good about the United States. As he writes in his book *Violence over the Land*, "Reconciling the dispossession of millions with the making of America remains a sobering challenge, an endeavor that requires reevaluation of many enduring historical assumptions. A generation of scholars has already begun this large task, and this book aims to contribute to it."[22] As does this one.

"INDIANS SHOULD MOVE ON AND FORGET THE PAST"

Dina relates the story of an experience she once had:

> Many years ago I had an eye-opening conversation with a person who was at the time my employer, someone who by most standards would be considered highly educated. We were discussing the possibility of an Indian casino being built in our town, at the time a very contentious and divisive issue in the community. I was pro-casino and he was con. Our conversation veered off into the territory of the historical injustice that today's Indian nations face and that gave rise to the law that regulates Indian gaming. Smugly and with an air of righteousness he said, "Indians should just accept the fact that there was a war and they lost," seeming oblivious to the fact that he was talking to one of those Indians. I was shocked at his insensitivity and not sure how to respond. It was the first time I remember coming face to face with the sentiment, but it was definitely not the last.

Like many of the myths covered in this book, the idea that Indians should forget the past is multilayered. In this case, as Dina's employer's proclamation reflects, the implication is that Indians have failed to accept a fundamental fact about history (they were conquered) and are sore losers, as if they had lost an election or a game of poker. Indians are expected to flow seamlessly (if not happily) into the civic and political landscape of the United States and let go of their cultures, their homelands, and their very identities. The myth of being conquered is encompassed by a larger myth—that Indians are stuck in the past and that by holding on to their identities they fail to function in the world as modern people.

The reality is far more complex than winning and losing, or being stuck in the past. To embrace and perpetuate a narrative of conquest as a defining feature of the US relationship with American Indian nations is to exhibit an extremely limited understanding of that history in general, and of federal Indian law in particular. Additionally, the meaning of "conquest" in this line of reasoning is predicated on the idea that might makes right. It is used to serve a political agenda that justifies the violence of the settler state, taking for granted the philosophy of manifest destiny as though it is a natural law of the universe. There is an unconscious adherence to manifest destiny in the writing of US history, a default position and "trap of a mythological unconscious belief" in the idea.[1]

Indeed, after the 1840s, when the phrase "manifest destiny" was first coined and incorporated into the national vernacular, it gained so much currency that it was rarely questioned until the advent of the Indian rights movement of the 1960s and 1970s.[2] The concept of conquest did find its way into the federal legal system in 1823 with the notorious *Johnson v. M'Intosh* Supreme Court ruling—laying the foundation for the vast body of federal Indian law with the articulation of the doctrine of discovery and preparing fertile ground for the seeds of manifest destiny and the roots of American exceptionalism. It was also made possible by fraud and collusion within the US court system.[3] However, from the beginning the relationship between American Indian nations and the United States was based on treaties, which by their very nature are characterized by the recognition of mutual sovereignty. Since the 1820s Native people have without their consent been subject to a foreign system of law so rife with conflict and contradiction that it has been described as "schizo-phrenic" and "at odds with itself."[4] In short, the doctrine of dis-covery (and its offspring, the myth of conquest) is only one legal principle among numerous others that make up the complex labyrinth of federal Indian law. By considering it in the context of other competing legal doctrines, we can see why "conquest" is a misnomer that conceals other salient principles that sup-port the opposite of conquest, which is sovereignty.

Even though *Johnson v. M'Intosh* didn't involve Indians di-rectly, it is generally considered to be the first legal precedent to begin intervening in the lives of Indian people. The deci-sion, penned by Chief Justice John Marshall, articulated the concept that "discovery" by the culturally and religiously "su-perior" Christian Europeans constituted conquest, but it did so in a way that admitted the pompousness of the claim. Marshall even went so far as to say that "however extravagant the *preten-tion of converting the discovery of an inhabited country into conquest* may appear [emphasis added]; if the principle has been as-serted in the first instance, and afterwards sustained; if a coun-try has been acquired and held under it; if the property of the great mass of the community originates in it, it becomes the law of the land, and cannot be questioned."[5]

It has been noted that many scholars believe the purpose of the *Johnson* decision was to "craft a rational scheme for land ac-quisition in the United States," but the fact that the decision had catastrophic effects would become clear almost immediately as it became instrumental in Andrew Jackson's removal policy, leading to the Trail of Tears.[6]

In 1832, on the other hand, Marshall appeared to backpedal from the *Johnson* decision when in *Worcester v. Georgia* he ruled that tribes were "distinct political communities, having territo-rial boundaries, within which their authority is exclusive." Na-tive nations, said Marshall, paraphrased by David E. Wilkins, "retained enough sovereignty to exclude the states from exercising any power over Indian peoples or their territories."[7] The *Worcester* decision gave rise to the concept of tribal sovereignty and is one of the bedrock principles of federal Indian law today. It is important to understand, as many scholars and legal experts argue, however, that tribal sovereignty is not a right granted by US law, but that it is inherent in the treaty relationship. The idea of conquest is, therefore, one among numerous legal fictions that today make up the federal Indian law canon.

Like the myth of conquest, the concept of modernity is vexed, presenting a "modern/traditional dichotomy" for Indigenous peoples, as Colleen O'Neill writes.[8] This dichotomy presumes a universalist and linear view of human development rooted in the European Enlightenment, where all humans are seen to progress from stages of barbarity to civilization (also known as the theory of "natural law" by philosophers Thomas Hobbes, John Locke, and others). In this model, American Indians, as "backward" and "uncivilized," are seen as an impediment to progress, and indeed all US Indian policy has been based on this philosophy. O'Neill argues that "modernity" is really code for "capitalist development" and that many American Indians have adapted to the capitalist system in ways that infuse cultural values and tradition with modernity. Examples include Tlingit fishermen in Alaska, who adopted the commercial salmon industry in ways that "did not necessarily undermine their subsistence practices," and the development among Navajo women of a market for their wool rugs.[9] The same can be said for the rise of the Indian gaming industry, and many other examples too numerous to name illustrate the ways Fourth World peoples transcend the modern/traditional dichotomy in late capitalism.

Modernity signifies more than just adaptation to capitalism, however. Ojibwe scholar Scott Lyons believes that the "next big project" for Native American studies and the Indigenous movement more broadly is "to develop new ways of engaging with the irreducible *modernity* and *diversity* that inheres in every Native community and has for some time."[10] Lyons's point is that in today's Native communities on reservations (he draws on the example of his own reservation at Leech Lake in Minnesota), Native people are so diverse ethnically, religiously, politically, and culturally that it makes no sense to talk in terms of assimilation and authenticity (where the adaptation to the modern world is understood as assimilation, and authenticity is understood as adherence to a culturally "pure" past). He recognizes the existence of a binary in academic and activist discourses where modernity is juxtaposed to indigeneity, but he argues for "an embracement of indigenous modernity [that] requires a different relationship to the past, one that does not seek to go backward but instead attempts to bring the past forward."[11] This he sees as strengthening the decolonization project and articulated most strenuously in expressions of tribal nationalism, defined as "the politicization of culture for the achievement of national goals, such as land rights and sovereignty." It is the modernization of ancient tribal nations and is ultimately a form of resistance to oppression.

But what about Indian people who live outside their home reservation communities, as the majority of Native people today do? How do they maintain Native identities without succumbing to the modern/traditional dichotomy or Lyons's modernity/indigeneity binary? Just as in reservation communities, they do it not only by "bringing the past forward" but by adapting the past to the present in ways that appeal to the common interests and characteristics of the wide diversity of Native people in large urban centers, in what is sometimes called "pan-Indianism." Pan-Indian practices include powwows and certain spiritual traditions like the sweat lodge and pipe ceremonies. Religious studies scholar Dennis F. Kelley contends that historically for non-Indians this pan-Indian identity was a marker of modernity that signaled a stage in the elimination of Indianness altogether on the road to assimilation, but that it was in fact—and still is—a tool for resistance to assimilation.[12] For Native people who grow up in large cities, participating in powwows and other pan-Native cultural activities is the road back to their particular tribal identities, or what Kelley calls cultural "reprise."[13] In this way, "Indian country" is not limited to reservation boundaries but is defined as the places where Indian people gather. At powwows, for example, even though they might take place in white-dominated spaces and there may be many non-Native people in attendance, it is Indian protocol (worldview, knowledge, rules, history, etc.) that controls the powwow space—with all its modern adaptations.

Indian people can be seen in all walks of modern life bringing their Nativeness with them. From the world of modern cinema, where people like Chris Eyre (director and coproducer of the movie *Smoke Signals*) and Neil Diamond (*Reel Injuns*) are helping to reshape the distorted contours of a notoriously racist industry, to the political arena, where Indian people like Ben Nighthorse Campbell and Tom Cole exercise influence in public discourse, Indigenous people bring their identities with them. Astronaut John Harrington (Chickasaw) became the first Native American to fly into space, making his Indigenous mark on science. A member of the sixteenth shuttle mission to the International Space Station in 2002, Harrington carried with him six eagle feathers, a braid of sweetgrass, two arrowheads, and the Chickasaw Nation flag. Professional sports has been a terrain of modern achievement for Indians from Jim Thorpe to Navajo professional golfer Notah Begay. Even in what some might think of as the whitest of cultural spaces, surfing, which originated with Native Hawaiians, Native people can be found bringing their cultures with them. Take the case of the late surfer and surfboard shaper Johnny Rice (Prairie Band Potawatomie). Rice was known in surfing circles for his commitment to the Sundance tradition and often talked about surfing being similar to the four directions because of its ability to balance a person mentally, emotionally, physically, and spiritually. All of these individuals remind US Americans that Indians are more than relics of a bygone past. They are people with vibrant, relevant cultures who are here to stay.

"Europeans Brought Civilization to the Backward Indians"

"Behind each successful man stands a woman and behind each policy and program with which Indians are plagued, if traced completely back to its origin, stands the anthropologist," wrote Vine Deloria Jr. in 1969, with the snarky tone that characterized so much of his work.

> The fundamental thesis of the anthropologist is that people are objects for observation; people are then considered objects for experimentation, for manipulation, and for eventual extinction. The anthropologist thus furnishes the justification for treating Indian people like so many chessmen available for anyone to play with.
>
> The massive volume of useless knowledge produced by anthropologists attempting to capture real Indians in a network of theories has contributed substantially to the invisibility of Indian people today.[1]

Deloria's issue with academia—and anthropology in particular—was essentially that it was irrelevant to the problems of everyday Indians. It failed to meet the needs created by rampant poverty and the never-ending encroachment of settlers into Indian lands. Anthropologists' work set traps for Indian people and rendered them invisible when they didn't conform to stereotyped images of dancing Indians or Indians forever on the warpath. Deloria wrote, "The conclusion has been reached—Indians must be redefined in terms that white men will accept, even if that means re-Indianizing them according to a white man's idea of what they were like in the past and should logically become in the future."[2]

Picking up where Deloria left off, Robert Berkhofer scathingly critiqued non-Natives' obsession with defining Indians in *The White Man's Indian*.[3] Berkhofer traced the excruciating history of what is commonly called "scientific racism," building on Reginald Horsman's oft-cited 1975 article "Scientific Racism and the American Indian in the Mid-Nineteenth Century."[4] Scientific racism, like the Bering Strait land bridge theory, has deep roots in Christian theology and is connected to the concept of manifest destiny. Manifest destiny was first articulated as the guiding principle for US expansionism, underpinned by Euro-American ethnocentrism and the imperative of Christian fundamentalists to save the Indian soul. The "white man's burden" was based on a deeply entrenched ideology of the racial inferiority of nonwhite peoples, which by the 1880s had been shored up by evolving social Darwinist theories. That all nonwhite peoples were inferior was a given, accepted as fact among religious fundamentalists as well as secular intellectuals and scientists.

Emerging scientific theories in the eighteenth and nineteenth centuries came to explain human diversity in terms of evolution and progress, and some humans were seen as innately more advanced than others and thus superior. This was expressed in the scientific terms "monogenesis" and "polygenesis." Monogenesis—the theory that all humankind descended from an original pair—found itself contending with polygenesis, the idea that human diversity could be explained by "the separate creation of individual races."[5] Embracing the latter idea,

Samuel George Morton and his disciples in what had become known as the "American School" of ethnology had scientifically "proven" the superiority of the white race based on comparative cranium measurements of white, black, Australian Aborigine, and Indian skulls. The results of their study of several hundred skulls, in which average cranium measurements were smaller for non-Caucasians, were correlated to the supposed barbarity of non-Caucasians. Published in 1854, the eight-hundred-page *Types of Mankind: Or, Ethnological Researches*, by Morton follower J. C. Nott, summarized that

intelligence, activity, ambition, progression, high anatomical development characterize some races; stupidity, indolence, immobility, savagism, low anatomical development characterize others. Lofty civilization, in all cases has been achieved solely by the "Caucasian" group. Mongolian races, save in the Chinese family, in no instance have reached beyond the degree of semi-civilization; while the Black races of Africa and Oceania no less than the Barbarous tribes of America have remained in utter darkness for thousands of years. . . .

Furthermore, certain savage types can neither be civilized nor domesticated. The Barbarous races of America (excluding the Toltecs) although nearly as low in intellect as the Negro races, are essentially untameable. Not merely have all attempts to civilize them failed, but also every endeavor to enslave them. Our Indian tribes submit to extermination, rather than wear the yoke under which our Negro slaves fatten and multiply.

It has been falsely asserted, that the Choctaw and Cherokee Indians have made great progress in civilization. I assert positively, after the most ample investigation of the facts, that the pureblooded Indians are everywhere unchanged in their habits. Many white persons, settling among the above tribes, have intermarried with them; and all such trumpeted progress exists among these whites and their mixed breeds alone. The pureblooded savage still skulks untamed through the forest, or gallops athwart the prairie. Can any one call the name of a single pure Indian of the Barbarous tribes who—except in death, like a wild cat—has done anything worthy of remembrance?[6]

Nott was a staunch defender of slavery, and his polemics are on the extreme end of scientific racism. His work was nonetheless on a spectrum of scientific thought that constructed categories of humans based on biological characteristics that could be used to explain cultural differences and that provided "the rationale for the exploitation, appropriation, domination, and dehumanization of people of color . . . sanctioned by the state."[7] In Nott's narrative, if there is to be redemption (framed as civilization or domestication) for "certain savage types"—in this case Indians—it is only through the racial blending with whites that this can occur. Intermarriage between Indians and whites is cast as the only possibility for progress for the Indian "race."[8] The argument was not a new one, and it was imperative for Indians to adopt other white practices. Thomas Jefferson, for instance, had argued in 1785, in *Notes on the State of Virginia*, that if Indians adopted European-style agriculture, gave up hunting as a subsistence lifestyle, and lived in European-style towns they could advance from savagery to civilization. The shift to a sedentary life would also conveniently free up the hunting grounds and facilitate white settlement with greater ease, and presumably intermarrying with whites would contribute to their elevation.

The bigotry inherent in science, in other words, provided the intellectual justification for the social hierarchies that kept all people of color culturally and legally subordinated to dominant white society well into the twentieth century, and laid the foundation for federal Indian policy, especially the assimila-tionist project of the Dawes Act (General Allotment Act) from 1887 to 1934, which authorized the division of Indian land into individually owned allotments. The philosophical tenets of as-similation held that Indians could advance from their perceived savage state to civilization through farming, private ownership of land, and formal, European-style education.⁹ The philosophy was embraced not only by those openly hostile to Indians but also by Indian advocates, white "friends of Indians" who saw assimilation policy as the most compassionate approach in the face of aggressive white settlement. Promoting assimilation was one of many techniques the federal government used for ethnic cleansing, removing Indigenous people from their land and as-suring their disappearance by absorbing them into the US citi-zenry. In the end, true to the imperative of settler colonialism to gain access to Indigenous territories, it turned out to be a mas-sive land grab by the United States, with a loss of two-thirds of Indian treaty lands by an act of legislation.

It might be tempting to think that by applying the term "rac-ism" to the social Darwinist philosophies of the eighteenth and nineteenth centuries we are unfairly judging yesterday by to-day's standards because we now presumably live in a different, more just world. The problem, however, is that where American Indians are concerned the prejudice that defined the past has woven itself into the present through the vast and bewildering body of federal Indian law, in what legal scholar Robert A. Wil-liams unapologetically referred to as the racist language of the US Supreme Court. Williams explores in vivid detail the court's development and use of the Marshall Trilogy (three cases from the 1820s and 1830s, *Johnson v. M'Intosh*, *Cherokee Nation v. Georgia*, and *Worcester v. Georgia*), whose reliance upon the rac-ist language regarding Indian "savagery" and cultural inferior-ity maintains a system of legalized white racial dictatorship over

Indian tribes even today. Williams writes, "As evidenced by their own stated opinions on Indian rights, a long legacy of hostile, romanticized, and incongruously imagined stereotypes of Indians as incommensurable savages continues to shape the way the justices view and understand the legal history, and therefore the legal rights, of Indian tribes."[10] Beginning in 1823 with *Johnson v. M'Intosh*, considered by Williams to be by far the most important Indian rights opinion ever issued in the United States, the racist language of Indian savagery was institutionalized in the Supreme Court: "The tribes of Indians inhabiting this country were fierce savages, whose occupation was war." With Justice Marshall's words several things were accomplished: the precedent for all subsequent Indian cases was set; the taking of Indian land based upon racial, cultural, and religious superiority of Europeans was justified; and language was codified that would justify future federal incursions into Indian lives and resources.

References to Indian savagery occurred many times in subsequent nineteenth-century Supreme Court decisions, in cases such as *United States v. Rogers* (1846), *Ex Parte Crow Dog* (1883), and *United States v. Kagama* (1886). While the tradition of racist language in the court reared its ugly head in African American cases as well, most famously in *Dred Scott v. Sanford* (1856) and later in *Plessy v. Ferguson* (1896), the twentieth century saw a paradigm shift with *Brown v. Board of Education* (1954), the landmark decision credited as heralding the civil rights movement a decade later. Yet when it came to Indian rights cases, the language of white racial superiority was still very much alive in *Tee-Hit-Ton v. United States* (1955) and even into the Rehnquist Court with *Oliphant v. Suquamish Indian Tribe* (1978) and *United States v. Sioux Nation of Indians* (1980). The entire body of federal Indian law is based on nineteenth-century precedents and outmoded ways of thinking, yet this is tolerated if not staunchly defended by those in power. Historically, when the justices of the Supreme Court have chosen to reject the language of prior decisions (the practice of *stare decisis*)—decisions that only served to oppress certain peoples—and adapt a new language that affirms their rights, positive paradigm shifts have occurred within the court and society at large.

"THE UNITED STATES DID NOT HAVE A POLICY OF GENOCIDE"

Chiitaanibah Johnson, a nineteen-year-old of Navajo and Maidu ancestry, was a sophomore English major at Sacramento State University in September 2015 when she got into an intellectual tussle with her American history professor one day in class. In a lecture about California Indian history, the part-time adjunct professor, Maury Wiseman, claimed that he did not like the term "genocide" when describing Native American history, believing it "too strong a word for what happened" and saying that "genocide implies that it was on purpose and most native people were wiped out by European diseases."[1] Over the next couple of days of ongoing class discussions and Johnson producing evidence for genocide, Wiseman contended that she had hijacked his class and was accusing him of bigotry and racism.[2] Claims emerged that he had subsequently disenrolled her from the class (claims that were disputed), triggering an investigation into the incident. The result of the university's investigation found no one at fault.

The story quickly infiltrated online news outlets and social media, sparking heated debates about Native American history and whether or not the word "genocide" accurately characterizes the American Indian experience, or more to the point, US treatment of Indians. Among professional and lay historians few topics can elicit the kind of emotional charge that discussions about genocide can. Conventional exceptionalist historical narratives that celebrate the United States as the beacon of democracy and human rights in the world are, after all, diametrically opposed to those that implicate the United States in the "crime of crimes" alongside Nazi Germany, the Ottoman Empire (Armenian Genocide), the Rwandan Hutus, and others. It wasn't until the second half of the twentieth century, with the rise of the civil rights movement, the birth of ethnic and native studies programs, and increasing entrance of people of color into higher education that scholars began applying the term "genocide" to the US policies, even though the term "extermination" was widely used throughout the nineteenth century and earlier when referring to US policies regarding Indians.

After several unsuccessful attempts to pass legislation issuing a formal apology to Native Americans, in 2009 a bill was passed without fanfare, having been slipped quietly—and ironically—into a defense appropriations bill. The joint resolution acknowledges historical events like the massacres at Wounded Knee and Sand Creek, forced removals of entire nations from their homelands, and the taking of children from their families for education in distant boarding schools. It acknowledges "years of official depredations, ill-conceived policies, and the breaking of covenants by the Federal Government regarding Indian tribes" and expresses "regret for the ramifications of former wrongs." But nowhere is the word "genocide" used. In fact, as if to minimize US violence against Natives, one sentence mentions Native violence: "Natives and non-Native settlers engaged in numerous armed conflicts in which unfortunately, both took innocent lives, including those of women and children." The inclusion of this clause problematically decontextualizes the reality of counterinsurgency-style warfare that the United States and earlier European settlers exercised against Native peoples, which ultimately killed far more Natives than non-Natives.[3]

Debates on whether or not genocide occurred on US soil follow several different tracks and depend largely upon how narrowly or loosely "genocide" is defined. The most common method among historians who argue against it is to compare the Native American experience to other genocides, the Jewish Holocaust in particular. Along this line of analysis, as Lyman Legters points out, the problem with too expansive a definition is that diluting the criteria for genocide too much renders its definition meaningless.[4] On the other hand, as Legters argues, if the definition of genocide is limited to the "actual mass killing of victim peoples," it blurs the concept of genocide as a crime by diminishing "those practices directed against whole peoples or other definable social groups with the effect of destroying their integrity as groups," in what is called cultural genocide. Even the term "cultural genocide," Legters argues, is problematic because it obscures "the seriousness obviously intended in the campaign to make genocide a crime." A. Dirk Moses, author of a study based on Australia's colonial experience, contends that regarding genocide as synonymous with the Jewish Holocaust discourages comparative genocide studies. Moses suggests instead that thinking of genocide as extreme counterinsurgency aids in understanding how colonial violence unfolds.[5]

Another common argument detractors use to refute the genocide contention is the one used by the Sacramento State professor: that it was disease that killed off most of the Indigenous population, not violence. As scholar Benjamin Madley writes, the argument that the dramatic decline of Native populations was due primarily to the "natural disaster" of biological pathogens has been so widely perpetuated that it has become a standard trope among historians.[6] One of its biggest problems is that it also promulgated the myth of an unoccupied virgin wilderness imagined by early settlers that justified their continual encroachment into Native territories.

A third and more moderate line of analysis holds that the term "genocide" may not necessarily apply to all American

Indian groups but might more appropriately be assessed on a group-by-group or region-by-region basis (a concept we'll return to momentarily). In order to make an accurate assessment of genocide, there must also be evidence of the deliberate intent of a state or government to annihilate an entire population. In the academic world, despite resistance during the 1970s and early 1980s within some disciplines to grant platforms to the study of genocide, the field of comparative genocide studies coalesced in 1994 with the founding of the International Association of Genocide Scholars. After reciting a comprehensive genealogy of the Native American genocide literature, Madley points out that genocide is more than an academic study since it is a crime under international law, framed by a treaty and subsequent case law.

Genocide was first legally defined in 1948 with the United Nations Convention on Genocide (Resolution 260 [III] of the General Assembly) in the wake of the Jewish Holocaust. One hundred forty-six member states, including the United States, are signatories to the convention. Raphaël Lemkin was a Polish legal scholar who escaped the Holocaust and emigrated to the United States, and it was he who coined and defined the term "genocide" in 1944 as it was adopted in the UN convention. According to the text of the treaty, "In the present Convention, genocide means any of the following acts committed with intent to destroy, in whole or in part, a national, ethnical, racial or religious group, as such:

  a. Killing members of the group;
  b. Causing serious bodily or mental harm to members of the group;
  c. Deliberately inflicting on the group conditions of life calculated to bring about its physical destruction in whole or in part;

d. Imposing measures intended to prevent births within the group;

e. Forcibly transferring children of the group to another group."

The description constitutes two aspects of genocide, physical (each of the five criteria) and mental ("the intent to destroy"). According to the organization Prevent Genocide International, "It is a crime to plan or incite genocide, even before killing starts, and to aid or abet genocide: Criminal acts include conspiracy, direct and public incitement, attempts to commit genocide, and complicity in genocide."[7] In the US context, the forcible transfer of children throughout the Indian boarding school era and the extent of transracial Indian adoption in the nineteenth and twentieth centuries alone arguably count as genocidal intent, even if no other criteria are considered.[8] Yet even if we accept conservative arguments against US genocidal intent against all Indian groups as a whole and assess it on a regional basis, California stands out as an exceptional site of genocidal intent, according to the research of Brendan C. Lindsay.

Lindsay draws upon the UN genocide convention to defend claims of full-scale genocide in his award-winning 2014 book *Murder State: California's Native American Genocide, 1846–1873*. For Lindsay, it is "not an exercise in presentism to employ the [UN] Convention as a model in a study of genocide for a period well before its creation" because the roots of genocide go deep into the historical past.[9] Even though the term "genocide" did not exist in nineteenth century California, the concept of "extermination" was well developed and widely deployed throughout the state. Citizen militias were empowered to murder Indians via a legal system that offered Indians no protection and rendered their existence basically illegal. The same legal structure had allowed the existence of a system of Indian slavery disguised as "apprenticeship." Recent research affirming Lindsay's findings has revealed that after 1846 at least twenty thousand California Indians worked in some form of bondage under non-Natives.[10] Lindsay contends that "by separating families, depriving children of Native linguistic and cultural education, and inflicting mental and physical hardships, Euro-Americans destroyed Native families, lowered birthrates, and committed physical, cultural, and economic genocide."[11]

Lindsay's research finds that "rather than a government orchestrating a population to bring about the genocide of a group, the population orchestrated a government to destroy a group."[12] As Lindsay writes,

While California had a state militia, it was the legally organized, heavily armed local volunteer units that committed most of the murders needed to speed up the dispossession and destruction of California Native peoples. These men, often elevated to the status of local heroes, served as the most violently effective tool of a democracy aroused against Native Americans: citizen-soldiers engaged in acts of self-interest disguised as self-preservation.[13]

The California gold rush had inspired a state-supported philosophy of extermination that only recently has acceptably begun to be referred to as genocide in the scholarship on California Indian history.[14] Lindsay's remarkable study, gathered from copious documentation of the era, argues that a full-scale genocidal campaign was waged against California Indians between 1846 and 1873. Carried out largely by citizen soldiers in "roving death squads known as volunteer companies," the extermination of Native people was driven initially not only by the gold rush and the imperative of manifest destiny but increasingly by the changing values of gold and land.[15] As the gold rush failed to live up to the expectations of immigrant miners, land came to be more important than gold. As Indians were pushed out of their traditional territories because of a flood of white settlement and encroachment into Native territories, they resisted and fought back in multiple ways to protect their lives, lands, cultures, and sovereignty. Self-defense was construed by settlers as aggression, and the deeply entrenched ideology of Indian inferiority meant that settlers considered California Indians as little more than animals. This dehumanization paved the way for the bloodbath that took place during the second half of the nineteenth century all over California.

Finally, Lindsay writes in no uncertain terms,

A key to understanding the relationships between Native Americans and non-Natives in California is to recognize that our shared past contains a genocide of monstrous character and proportions, perpetrated by democratic, freedom-loving citizens in the name of democracy, but really to secure great wealth in the form of land against Indians cast as savage, uncivilized, alien enemies. . . . We Californians are the beneficiaries of genocide.[16]

Around the same time that Chiitaanibah Johnson was battling her professor at Sacramento State about genocide, the topic of whether or not genocide took place in California was being debated with the Catholic Church's imminent canonization of Father Junipero Serra. Serra had been beatified in 1988, earning him the offical title of "blessed," one step on the road to canonization, the declaration of sainthood. Potential saints must demonstrate holiness through particular types of godly works and verified miracles. Serra qualified for sainthood, the Vatican argued, based on his extensive evangelizing among American Indians in California, when he founded the California mission system in the eighteenth century. He was held up as a model for today's Hispanics, spokesmen for the Vatican said.[17] But to the descendants of the Indians he converted, Serra was hardly the sort who should qualify for sainthood.

Native scholars and activists have long known about the abuses of the Catholic Church and publicly spoke of these and denounced them in 2004 when Senator Barbara Boxer sponsored a bill to provide $10 million of federal tax money to restore twenty-one crumbling California missions. Signed into law by George W. Bush in November that year, the California Mission Preservation Act was criticized by many as part of Bush's notorious and unconstitutional faith-based agenda.[18] The mission bill performed the work of not only stimulating the California tourist economy but of perpetuating the always romanticized image of the California mission era, a time California Indians consider as the beginning of the brutality their ancestors would face for the next century and a half, beginning with the Spanish padres under Father Serra.

As Lindsay noted, among historians the term "genocide" had been unacceptable in the scholarly literature until the 1970s, when the tide began to change, and the deeply entrenched habit of romanticizing the missions had not allowed for the characterization of slavery by the Catholic Church. In 1978, however, historian Robert Archibald controversially called attention to mission history by blatantly referring to it as a system of slavery, comparing it to the "forced movement of black people from Africa to the American South," making the connection between forced labor and Spanish economic self-interest. He argued that under the Spanish there was little distinction between the secular and the religious because of "a vested interest in economic exploitation of natives possible within the system. Too often economic exploitation of native peoples was the strongest foundation of the surrounding civilian and military society."[19]

In 2004 Elias Castillo, a three-time Pulitzer Prize nominee, wrote an op-ed for the *San Francisco Chronicle* criticizing the mission preservation bill and describing the missions as "little more than death camps run by Franciscan friars where thousands of California's Indians perished."[20] Castillo said that the editorial prompted him to write the book *A Cross of Thorns: The Enslavement of California Indians by the Mission System*, which wasn't released until January 2015, well into the Serra canonization crusade. *A Cross of Thorns* is a frontal assault on the Church's mission history and helped shore up the California Indian movement to oppose Serra's sainthood. The movement coalesced with a petition urging Pope Francis to abandon his canonization plans, signed by over ten thousand people.[21] With the pope's travels to South America and his apology to Indigenous peoples for the historic mistreatment of them by the Church, a glimmer of hope was raised that he might be persuaded to change his mind. That hope was dashed, however, when despite widespread criticism the elaborate canonization ceremony proceded unabated in Washington, DC, in September 2015. The Church stood up for Serra's work, claiming that it was unfair to judge Serra for his actions by today's standards, and it contended that the friar had protected the Indians.[22]

"US Presidents Were Benevolent or at Least Fair-Minded Toward Indians"

Indians and wolves are both beasts of prey,
tho' they differ in shape.

—George Washington

If ever we are constrained to lift the hatchet against any tribe,
we will never lay it down till that tribe is exterminated,
or driven beyond the Mississippi. . . . [I]n war, they will
kill some of us; we shall destroy them all.

—Thomas Jefferson

Established in the midst of another and a superior race,
and without appreciating the causes of their inferiority or seeking
to control them, they [the tribes] must necessarily yield to the force
of circumstances and ere long disappear.

—Andrew Jackson[1]

The myth of benevolent, fair-minded presidents derives from denial of the policy of genocide upon which the founding of the United States was based. After a decade of war, the British conceded independence to the colonists. In the 1783 Treaty of Paris, they transferred ownership of all British territory south of the Great Lakes, from the Mississippi to the Atlantic, and north of Spanish-occupied Florida, a much larger area than the thirteen colonies.

However, before the promulgation of the Constitution in 1787 and subsequent election of the first president, the elite of the thirteen insurgent British colonies issued a genocidal policy in the Northwest Ordinance. This was the first law of the incipient republic, revealing the motive for those desiring independence. It was the blueprint for occupying and driving out the substantial agricultural societies of the formerly British-protected Indian Territory ("Ohio Country") on the other side of the Appalachians and Alleghenies. Britain had made settlement there illegal with its Proclamation of 1763.

The Northwest Ordinance was a policy document based on the Land Ordinance of 1785 that had established a national system for surveying and marketing plots of land, and as historian Woody Holton has noted, "Under the May 1785 ordinance, Indian land would be auctioned off to the highest bidder."[2] The Northwest Ordinance, albeit containing rhetoric about guaranteeing Native occupancy and title, set forth an evolutionary colonization procedure for annexation via military occupation, territorial status, and finally statehood, with the Pacific Ocean as the final western boundary. Conditions for statehood would be achieved when the settlers outnumbered the Indigenous population, which required decimation or forced removal of Indigenous populations. In this US system, unique among colonial powers, land became the most important exchange commodity for the accumulation of capital and building of the national treasury. To understand the genocidal policy of the US government, the centrality of land sales in building the economic base of US wealth and power must be seen.

The drawing up of maps for US continental colonization was preceded and accompanied by brutal wars of extermination by Anglo colonialists in seizing the Indigenous territories that became the thirteen colonies, and the Anglo-American colonists warring against Britain for independence didn't miss a beat during that decade of war in wiping out Indigenous communities on the peripheries of the colonies. Those Native nations in British North America that refused to support the separatist forces were marked for annihilation. For instance, in response to the decisions by five of the six Iroquois nations to stay neutral or join the British effort, General George Washington wrote instructions to Major General John Sullivan to take peremptory action against the Iroquois,

> to lay waste all the settlements around . . . that the country may not be merely *over-run* but *destroyed*. . . . [Y]ou will not by any means, listen to any overture of peace before the total ruin of their settlements is effected. . . . Our future security will be in their inability to injure us . . . and in the terror with which the severity of the chastisement they receive will inspire them.[3] [Emphasis in the original]

Sullivan replied, "The Indians shall see that there is malice enough in our hearts to destroy everything that contributes to their support."

A new element was added to the independent Anglo-American legal regime: treaty-making. The US Constitution specifically refers to Indigenous nations only once, but significantly, in Article 1, Section 8: "[Congress shall have power] to regulate Commerce with foreign Nations and among the several States, and with the Indian Tribes." In the federal system, in which all powers not specifically reserved for the federal government go to the states, relations with Indigenous nations are unequivocally a federal matter.

Although not mentioned specifically, Native peoples are implied in the Second Amendment. Male settlers had been required in the colonies to serve in militias during their lifetimes for the purpose of raiding and razing Indigenous communities, and later states' militias were used as "slave patrols." The Second Amendment, ratified in 1791, enshrined these irregular forces into law: "A well regulated Militia, being necessary to the security of a free State, the right of the people to keep and bear Arms, shall not be infringed." The continuing significance of that "freedom" specified in the Bill of Rights reveals the settler-colonialist cultural roots of the United States that appear even in the present as a sacred right.

US genocidal wars against Indigenous nations continued unabated in the 1790s and were woven into the very fabric of the new nation-state, continuing across the continent for the next hundred years. The fears, aspirations, and greed of Anglo-American land speculators and settlers on the borders of Indigenous territories perpetuated this warfare and influenced the formation of the US Army, much as the demands and actions of backcountry settlers had shaped the colonial militias in North America. Brutal counterinsurgency warfare would be the key to the army's destruction of the Indigenous peoples' civilizations in the Ohio Country and the rest of what was then called the Northwest over the first two decades of US independence.[4]

In 1803, the Jefferson administration, without consulting any affected Indigenous nation, purchased the French-claimed Louisiana Territory (formerly Spanish) from Napoleon Bonaparte. This territory comprised 828,000 square miles, and its addition doubled the size of the United States. The territory encompassed all or part of multiple Indigenous nations, including the Sioux, Cheyenne, Arapaho, Crow, Pawnee, Osage, and Comanche nations, among other peoples of the bison. It also included the area that would soon be designated Indian Territory (Oklahoma), the future site of the forced relocation of Indigenous peoples from east of the Mississippi. Fifteen future states would emerge from the taking: all of present-day Arkansas, Missouri, Iowa, Oklahoma, Kansas, and Nebraska; the part of Minnesota west of the Mississippi; most of North and South Dakota; northeastern New Mexico and North Texas; the portions of Montana, Wyoming, and Colorado east of the Continental Divide; and Louisiana west of the Mississippi River, including New Orleans. Except for the city of New Orleans, the lands had not yet been subjected to settler-colonialism. The territory pressed against lands occupied by Spain, including Texas and all the territory west of the Continental Divide to the Pacific Ocean. These would soon be next on the US annexation list.

Wealthy plantation operators in Virginia and the Carolinas were usurping Cherokee- and Muskogee-developed farmlands in what became Georgia and were intent on establishing themselves in the Mississippi Valley. Neither superior technology nor an overwhelming number of settlers made up the mainspring of the birth and development of the United States. Rather, the chief cause was the colonialist settler-state's willingness to eliminate whole civilizations of people in order to possess their land. The avatar for the ethnic cleansing of that vast territory in what is now the US South was Andrew Jackson, the seventh president, serving from 1829 to 1837. He began the project in 1801, initiating his Indian-killing military career as head of the Tennessee militia.

As the most notorious land speculator in western Tennessee, Jackson had enriched himself by acquiring a portion of the Chickasaw Nation's land. After his militia's brutal wars of annihilation against the Choctaws and Creeks (Muskogees), Jackson continued building his national military and political career by tackling the resistant Seminole Nation in what was then Spanish-occupied Florida, with successive presidents Jefferson and Madison turning a blind eye. For his bloody and illegal deeds (invading a foreign European country), President James Monroe made Jackson the military governor of Florida and a general in the US Army, beginning what are known as the three Seminole Wars. In 1836, during the second of these wars, US Army general Thomas S. Jesup captured the popular Anglo attitude toward the Seminoles: "The country can be rid of them only by exterminating them." By then Jackson was finishing his second term as one of the most popular presidents in US history to that date.

During Jackson's first year as president, he shepherded through Congress the Indian Removal Act, and during the rest of his tenure oversaw the massive forced relocations to Indian Territory (now Oklahoma) of the five large agricultural nations of the Southeast—the Cherokees, Choctaws, Chickasaws, Creeks, and Seminoles, a third to half of migrants dying on the long journeys. There is little doubt that Jackson was the single most destructive president for Native Americans, but it is essential to remember that the deeds he carried out before and during his presidency had been inscribed as policy of the US government from its inception. As the late Cherokee principal chief Wilma Mankiller wrote in her autobiography:

> The fledgling United States government's method of dealing with native people—a process that then included systematic genocide, property theft, and total subjugation—reached its nadir in 1830 under the federal policy of President Andrew Jackson. More than any other president, he used forcible removal to expel the eastern tribes from their land. From the very birth of the nation, the United States government truly had carried out a vigorous operation of extermination and removal. Decades before Jackson took office, during the administration of Thomas Jefferson, it was already cruelly apparent to many Native American leaders that any hope for tribal autonomy was cursed. So were any thoughts of peaceful coexistence with white citizens.[5]

The Southern slave owner elite that controlled the presidency for nearly all of the first half-century of the United States succeeded in instrumentalizing the removal of all Native nations east of the Mississippi. With the cotton baronies free of Indigenous inhabitants, the seat of political power moved north with the expansion of slavery into the territories being a growing division between north and south, leading to the bloody Civil War. But the administration of Abraham Lincoln continued the policy of Indian destruction under the banner of "free soil." Lincoln's campaign for the presidency had appealed to the vote of land-poor settlers who demanded that the government "open" Indigenous lands west of the Mississippi. They were called "free-soilers," in reference to cheap land free of slavery.

In Minnesota, which had become a nonslavery state in 1859, the Dakota people were on the verge of starvation by 1862. When they mounted an uprising to drive out the mostly German and Scandinavian settlers, Union army troops crushed the revolt, slaughtering Dakota civilians and rounding up several hundred men. Three hundred prisoners were sentenced to death, but upon Lincoln's orders to reduce the numbers, thirty-eight were selected at random to die in the largest mass hanging in US history. In the midst of war, Lincoln did not forget his free-soiler settler constituency that had raised him to the presidency. During the Civil War, with the Southern states unrepresented, Congress at Lincoln's behest passed the Homestead Act in 1862, as well as the Morrill Act, the latter transferring large tracts of Indigenous land to the states to establish land grant universities. The Pacific Railroad Act provided private companies with nearly two hundred million acres of Indigenous land. With these land grabs, the US government broke multiple treaties with Indigenous nations. Most of the Western territories, including Colorado, North and

South Dakota, Montana, Washington, Idaho, Wyoming, Utah, New Mexico, and Arizona, were delayed in achieving statehood because Indigenous nations resisted appropriation of their lands and outnumbered settlers. So the colonization plan for the West established during the Civil War was carried out over the following three decades of war and land grabs. Under the Homestead Act, 1.5 million homesteads were granted to settlers west of the Mississippi, comprising nearly three hundred million acres (a half-million square miles) taken from the Indigenous collective estates and privatized for the market. This dispersal of landless settler populations from east of the Mississippi served as an "escape valve," lessening the likelihood of class conflict as the Industrial Revolution accelerated the use of cheap immigrant labor.

Up until the 1849 establishment of the Department of Interior, "Indian affairs" fell under the Department of War (renamed Department of Defense in 1947).[6] The Constitution established the president of the United States as commander in chief of the armed forces. So over the first seven decades of the United States, making war and expanding from the original thirteen states across the continent to the Pacific, US presidents' relationship with Indigenous nations was war. War on Native nations did not end with the transfer to Interior but rather continued for four decades, and the genocidal policy of elimination of the Native nations, as nations, is clear.

In 1871, Congress unilaterally ended Native nations' treaty-making power, an act that President Ulysses S. Grant did not challenge, although it was surely unconstitutional as a direct breach of the separation of powers doctrine. The result was the weakening of the US government's acknowledgment of Native nations' sovereignty. The role of the president was reduced to administrative powers regarding the Bureau of Indian Affairs and using executive orders to establish reservations. As Vine

Deloria Jr. noted, the president's role was reduced from that of a "negotiator of treaties to an administration of domestic disputes. . . . Indians as a subject of congressional debate were moved from the national agenda to an item on a committee agenda, and they were never again seen as having an important claim on national government."[7]

Since 1977, Native organizations and governments have been building institutional infrastructure and international human rights law within the United Nations. In 2007 this work produced the long-negotiated UN Declaration on the Rights of Indigenous Peoples, which calls for self-determination and a full range of specific and general human rights. There is a UN Special Rapporteur on Indigenous Peoples who monitors and reports on Indigenous complaints and government action in relation to the declaration. This has moved much Native American policy work from the Interior Department to the State Department and has led Native Americans to feel some optimism about future nation-building efforts.

"THE ONLY REAL INDIANS ARE FULL-BLOODS, AND THEY ARE DYING OFF"

At the core of narratives about Indian authenticity—particularly on the personal level—are popular assumptions about Indian "blood." They are made visible by the question "How much Indian blood do you have?"—asked inevitably by non-Native people of Native people or people who claim Native ancestry. At the root of the question, whether the questioner is cognizant of it or not, is an implicit demand to authenticate the claim. Is the percentage of Native ancestry sufficiently high? Whether or not the answer is acceptable may be based also on looks, clothing, or other situational elements. The hidden context is that a claim to Indian ancestry is automatically suspect since all the real Indians are presumed dead, or if there are any alive they are on a reservation. This is especially true in big cities, where Indians are invisible for a variety of reasons, not the least of which is because they can be easily mistaken for other ethnicities.[1] Among American Indians the "blood quantum" conversation is always contentious. It is contentious not only because it can mean the difference between being viewed by outsiders as authentically Native or conversely phony, but also because it can mean the difference between belonging and not belonging within Native communities or even within families. Unlike other ethnicities in the United States, American Indians are the only citizens who are subject to state-sanctioned legal definitions of identity, obligated to prove who they are as Indigenous peoples.

Native studies scholars talk about the dominant society's obsession with Indian authenticity as a fetishization of "blood," where blood is metaphorical, a stand-in for culture. A calculus where blood equals culture presupposes that genetics alone determines identity, absent other conditions such as upbringing, language, or other culturally specific markers of belonging outside dominant Euro-American society.[2] It emerges out of the history of scientific racism (discussed in myth 7), particularly where intermarriage was thought to improve (i.e., civilize) the inherently degraded "race." As Ryan Schmidt at the University of Montana writes, scientific racism linked physical characteristics with behavior, strengthening racial worldviews and creating social hierarchies. He points out that by the 1960s and 1970s, anthropologists had begun discarding systems of racial classification and had abandoned the validity of the concept of race.[3] Contemporary social scientists now widely affirm the idea of race as a social construction. Schmidt, like many scholars before him, traces the history of blood quantum as the arbiter of Indian identity, locating it throughout various eras of colonial and federal Indian policy, particularly as it was used during the period following enactment of the Dawes Act. This era "saw the concept of blood quantum become officially integrated into the legal status of Indian identity for the purposes of dividing communal tribal lands into individual parcels called allotments," whose ultimate purpose was to break up the communal lifestyles of Indigenous peoples.

The allotment policy connected Indian blood with competency (or lack thereof). Competency meant that an individual was capable of managing his or her own affairs, thus lifting a twenty-five-year restriction on the ability to sell an allotment (invariably resulting in more Indian land in white hands). Commissions that established competency equated competency with European ancestry. The more that European ancestry could determine the status of the allotments, the easier they would be to alienate, which served the US agenda to dispossess Indians of their lands. During this era tribes were encouraged to create rolls to determine tribal membership for the purpose of distributing allotments. Many scholars have argued that it was during this period that tribes internalized the blood quantum ideology in a process of being duped. Schmidt argues, however, that this is inaccurate since the federal government didn't force tribes to adopt blood quantum requirements, but rather advised them, providing them with step-by-step guidelines and charts on how they should determine blood quantum.[4] One study about allotment on the Colville reservation confirms the extent that tribal councils exercised their own will, influenced by their own cultural understandings about belonging and community membership. It demonstrates that in the early days (between 1906 and 1917), enrollment was more a function of perceptions of kinship and cultural affiliation than it was about adhering to the government's strictly defined blood quantum standards.[5]

In the bigger picture, however, the Colville example does reveal how blood quantum congealed as the prime determinant of tribal membership when in the 1937 base roll a one-eighth blood quantum requirement was established, which by 1939 had been changed again to one-quarter blood degree, where it remains today. This more restrictive and exclusionary criterion parallels the increasing commodification of Indian lands as tribal nations merged into a cash economy and came under the control of the Bureau of Indian Affairs. By the time tribes had become reconstituted under the Indian Reorganization Act of 1934, via corporate charters for the purpose of economic development, most tribal nations were extensions (or at least reflections) of the federal bureaucracy that oversaw them.[6] Tribes were now in the business of managing and distributing limited resources for which there had to be some way to divide a rapidly shrinking pie.[7] By and large, blood quantum became the default way to count who was and who was not deserving, even when it contradicted customary norms of Indigenous inclusion and identity. And it was complicated by the conditioning of boarding schools, which instilled a sense of shame about being Indian in the context of a white supremacist dominant social structure. Many denied their Indianness at times to avoid discrimination, while at other times they affirmed it for the benefits of land and other resources, often leaving behind impossibly tangled genealogical webs of documentation for future generations to sort out.

A solid body of federal Indian case law has for decades affirmed the power of Native nations to decide their membership in whatever ways they choose, blood quantum or not. But an equally ample body of scholarship makes the case that if they continue to adhere to minimum blood quantum standards eventually there will be no Indians left, in what has been called "paper" or "statistical" genocide. This is because Indians marry outside their cultures more than any other ethnic group, resulting in multiracial and multiethnic children. What's more, even when Indians have children with other Indians but from different tribes, it lowers the blood quantum necessary to enroll in one tribe (a requirement written into most tribal constitutions). It's possible for a person to have one half or more Indian blood combined from two or more tribes but not be able to enroll in any one tribe if they can't prove the tribally specific minimum blood degree—which is often one-quarter or one-half—or if the minimum blood degree derives from the wrong parent.[8] Some tribes, for instance, will only enroll children with maternal ancestry, while others will enroll only children with paternal ancestry, regardless of blood degree. Or a person can have a high degree of Indian blood from a tribe that has had federal recognition terminated (which happened to over one hundred tribes in the 1950s and 1960s). While he or she may self-identify as American Indian, the person won't be legally defined as such, resulting in ineligibility for federal benefits, whereas someone with much lower blood quantum could be eligible. Some Native nations are turning to genetic testing to assist them in their enrollment procedures.[9] This is not the magic bullet it's made out to be, however, because, for one thing, no test can determine the precise tribes from whom one has descended.[10]

For these reasons and more, scholars increasingly call on tribes to rethink their enrollment criteria. Seen through the lens of settler colonialism, blood quantum is the ultimate tool of Native elimination, but when tribes themselves employ it, it is self-imposed erasure. Native nations are gradually changing their practices, however. Some tribes have moved to accept all Indian blood in their blood quantum calculations for enrollment (the Colvilles among them). Other tribes have lowered the blood quantum minimums. The Ojibwes at White Earth are a recent high-profile example: in 2013 the tribe adopted a new constitution that changed a requirement for one-quarter blood quantum to lineal descent from an enrolled ancestor, with no minimum blood quantum required. Overall, the move toward definition by lineal descent is increasing. One 2011 study found that 42 percent of tribes are now utilizing a lineal descent rule, which is up from 15 percent using a lineal descent rule prior to 1940.[11]

Native scholars stress that the blood quantum system is foreign to ways Indigenous peoples historically determined community membership. In most tribal nations, individuals could be incorporated from outside through capture, adoption, or intermarriage, where belonging was a function of cultural participation and competence. Identity from an Indigenous perspective, in other words, is less a product of quantifiable biology than it is a function of kinship and culture, directly invalidating the popular myth that "real" Indians are only full-bloods who are dying off.[12]

"THE UNITED STATES GAVE INDIANS THEIR RESERVATIONS"

Of all the myths that surround American Indians, none is as confounding as the misunderstanding that the federal government gave Indians their lands. Arguably it derives from the conquest myth, which would have people believe that because of military domination (and later legal domination) whatever lands and rights Indian nations do enjoy are due to the "benevolent supremacy" of the US government.[1] Belief in the conquest myth and benevolence of the United States underscores the tenacity of the manifest destiny narrative, but it fails to change the actual reality that all of Turtle Island (the North American continent) has been Indian land since tens of thousands of years before European invasion. And it does not change the fact that it was Indians who gave up lands to the United States in treaties, not the other way around.

The word itself—"reservation"—refers to the lands that were reserved for Native nations after they ceded vast swaths of their territories to the United States through treaties. Land cessions were one of two primary functions of treaties, the other being to forge peace agreements. Today the federal government refers to three different types of reservations: military, public, and Indian. Indian reservations are lands that are held in trust for tribal nations by the federal government. According to the Bureau of Indian Affairs, 56.2 million acres of land are held in trust on behalf of tribal nations and individuals, with approximately 326 Indian land areas in the United States administered as federal Indian reservations, known variously as reservations, pueblos, rancherias, missions, villages, and communities.[2] Other types of Indian lands include allotted lands (individual allotments held in trust by the government) and state reservations, in which lands are held in trust for Indians by a state, not the federal government. Reservations were also created by executive order and congressional acts, and even though there are now 567 federally recognized tribal nations, not all nations have reservations. There is only one Indian reservation in Alaska (the Metlakatla Indian Community of the Annette Island Reserve in southeastern Alaska). Alaska Native groups are organized as corporations under the Alaska Native Claims Settlement Act of 1971, so while there are many Indigenous people in Alaska, their legal status is slightly different than American Indians in the lower forty-eight states.

Along with the myth that the federal government gave Indians their lands, there is another fiction that goes something like this: because Indian reservations are places of oppression they should be abolished. This fiction has been behind numerous disastrous policy decisions. The early days of the reservations (mid- to late-nineteenth century) were oppressive in many places—especially where subsistence lifestyles had been dependent upon hunting, like in the Great Plains—because of federal policies that restricted Indians to their reservation boundaries, which were often too small to allow a subsistence hunting lifestyle. In frequent cases, treaty-guaranteed annuities and food rations were never received, resulting in starvation and conditions of extreme poverty, especially as traditional political economies became supplanted by Euro-American capitalism.[3] Viewing traditional Native lifestyles as backward and uncivilized, the federal government enacted a policy of forced assimilation to break up communal landholdings and imposed a system of private property ownership through the General

Allotment Act of 1887 (the Dawes Act). The law turned out to be no more than a massive land grab for the United States that resulted in the loss of two-thirds of the lands reserved for Indians by treaties and increased reservation poverty rates. Poverty intensified also when the federal government embarked on a campaign to eradicate the massive buffalo herds on the plains (to force a sedentary lifestyle), and when Indians were defrauded out of their individual allotments, leaving many penniless and landless.

By the early twentieth century, a commission to study the deplorable conditions on the reservations found Indian poverty a direct result of failed government policies. The Meriam Report of 1928 recommended (among other things) that Native nations be allowed to be more self-governing, signaling a new policy direction, which would be manifest with the passage of the Wheeler-Howard Act (the Indian Reorganization Act) of 1934. While a step in the right direction, this still kept Indians tightly tethered to the paternalism of the US government.[4] Within twenty years, with the political winds blowing in a far more conservative direction under the postwar (and emerging Cold War) Eisenhower administration, Congress pushed for a new policy in a renewed attempt to forcibly assimilate Indians into mainstream society. This time assimilation was framed in terms of "liberating" Indians from the oppressive control of the federal government, which it proposed to do by eliminating the trust relationship, effectively freeing the United States from its own treaty obligations. House Concurrent Resolution 108 was passed in 1953 in an effort to abolish federal "supervision" over Indians. By eliminating the trust responsibility, the United States would terminate Indian reservations by converting them to private ownership once and for all.[5] Under HCR 108, Congress also established the relocation program—a jobs program that gave Indians a one-way ticket from their reservations to low-paying jobs in big cities such as Chicago, Los Angeles, San Francisco, Minneapolis, Seattle, and New York—all in an attempt to "negate Indian identity."[6] In the long run, relocation resulted in a wholesale population transfer, so that more Indians now live in cities than on reservations. The federal trust relationship was terminated for 109 tribes, affecting 1.3 million acres of Indian land (falling out of Indian hands) and an estimated twelve thousand Indians.[7]

The words "termination" and "relocation" to this day are enough to make an Indian's blood run cold. The Colville reservation is often looked to in termination studies as a case where termination was narrowly averted in a highly contentious twenty-year intra-tribal battle. Because tribes were allowed to vote on whether or not to accept termination, it is a study not only in the ways Native nations exercised choice but also a retrospective view on how disastrous termination was for so many, as it would have been for the Colvilles.[8] It illustrates that even with the problems associated with the federal trust relationship and the paternalistic nature of aboriginal title, reservations are still considered homelands for those who are born and raised there—and even for some who were not.

Accompanying the various assumptions about reservations as undesirable places that should be abandoned is another common belief related to Native authenticity and identity, that the only real Indians today are from reservations. The implication is that Native people who are from cities are not authentically Native, presumably because they are more acculturated to dominant white society (i.e., assimilated) and cut off from their Indigenous cultures of origin. Native scholars and writers have vigorously challenged this idea for generations, in both fiction and nonfiction. While reservations are geographic centers that link Native people to their Indigenous ancestry and historical continuity, Renya K. Ramirez conceptualizes urban Native spaces as "hubs" of culture that facilitate connections between reservations and cities. Such Native spaces include Indian centers, powwows, sweat lodges and other ceremonies, and any other kind of places and activities that gather Native people together in expressions of indigeneity.[9] In traveling between cities and reservations, Native identity is enacted and reinforced. Ramirez writes, "This constant movement and interaction disrupts the idea of Native cultural identity as a fixed, core essence. In contrast, urban Indian identity, according to the hub, is flexible and fluid. Thus, Native Americans' interactions with each other in the city and on the reservation can transform and rejuvenate tribal identity."[10]

As people living in diaspora, the hub emphasizes urban Indians' "strong rooted connection to tribe and homeland" and demonstrates the "potential for political power as Native men and women organize across tribal lines."[11] The Red Power movement of the 1960s and 70s, for instance—born out of the Alcatraz Island occupation in San Francisco and the formation of the American Indian Movement in the mean streets of Minneapolis—displays the way urban political organizing had far-reaching positive effects for both city and reservation Indians. Finally, the idea of hubs also applies to Indigenous conceptions of transnationalism (as opposed to pan-tribalism), where Indigenous nationhood is underscored. Sovereignty and self-determination are affirmed as political principles that differentiate Native peoples from other racial and ethnic groups, while it decenters the nation-state as the default arbiter of civic belonging and national identity.

"INDIANS ARE WARDS OF THE STATE"

In December 2014, Arizona Republican congressman Paul Gosar set off a tidal wave of controversy through Indian country when he referred to American Indian nations as "wards of the federal government." Gosar sponsored the Southeast Arizona Land Exchange and Conservation Act of 2013—a bill that opened up an Apache sacred site to copper mining—and his comment was made during a public meeting in Flagstaff to discuss it. According to an Associated Press report, during a roundtable discussion with a White Mountain Apache citizen who voiced his concerns about the land deal and proposed mine, Gosar retorted, "You're still wards of the federal government," implying not so subtly that what Indians want doesn't matter and that the federal government can do as it likes.[1]

Gosar's comment added insult to injury after a decade-long battle to protect the site known as Oak Flat, formerly Apache-owned land but now national forest, from mining development. His bill was a gift to Resolution Copper (whose parent company is the controversial British-Australian mining giant Rio Tinto), which had long been courting Congress for permission to mine the site, an action staunchly resisted by environmental and Native activists. Rio Tinto has a long record of human rights violations and egregious environmental practices dating back to the 1930s Spanish dictatorship of Francisco Franco. It is deeply implicated in the ongoing genocide of the Indigenous peoples of West Papua in Indonesia. The bill provided for the swap of five thousand acres "of overgrazed grassland, burned out forests and dry riverbeds in various parcels of land scattered around the state" held by Resolution Copper for twenty-four hundred acres of "forests, streams, desert, grasslands, craggy mountains, and huge rock formations with ancient petroglyphs."[2] The open pit mine will create a massive hole in the ground that will inevitably leave the site a toxic wasteland, as so many of Rio Tinto's projects have been known to do throughout the world.[3]

The land swap is a brutal example of the lack of sacred site protections that Fourth World nations in the United States still endure, and Gosar's remark was a slap in the face to the Apache people who use Oak Flat for traditional purposes like ceremonies and medicine gathering. Yet as offensive as it was, it did open up a public conversation about the "wards of the government" myth that is still so indelibly etched in the public imagination. It has become a cliché that can be bandied about callously in public battles between Congress and Indian country.[4]

The misnomer finds its origins in the nineteenth-century Supreme Court case *Cherokee Nation v. Georgia* (1831), part of the Marshall Trilogy (see myth 7), which forms the basis of today's body of federal Indian law. The court in the Marshall Trilogy cases of the 1820s and 1830s attempted to articulate a coherent approach for US dealings with Native nations at a time of relentless settler encroachment into Indian lands and a gradually shifting balance of military power. In *Cherokee Nation*, the court needed to decide how much authority states possessed to intervene in the affairs of Indians, which meant determining the nature of Indians' relationship to the United States and thus the nature of Indian sovereignty. Chief Justice Marshall claimed, "They may, more correctly, be denominated domestic dependent nations. They occupy a territory to which we assert a title independent of their will, which must take effect in point of possession, when their right of possession ceases. Meanwhile, they are in a state of pupilage; their relation to the United States resembles that of a ward to its guardian." Marshall did not explicitly define the relationship between Native nations and the federal government as a ward to its guardian, but used that—with exceptional hubris—as an analogy to describe the inferior status of the nations.[5] The *Cherokee* opinion (as with the Marshall Trilogy in general) was a blatant display of the growing US paternalism toward the nations and was the beginning of the eventual repudiation of the treaty-based relationship that had been in place from the country's beginning. If *Johnson v. M'Intosh* (1828) created the legal fiction known as the doctrine of discovery, which essentially legalized the concept of Indian inferiority, the wardship idea further bolstered it and has since been used by jurists and legislators in convoluted and manipulative ways to maintain dominance. For instance, when Indian Country Today Media Network asked for comments from Gosar about his statement, his reply was that "the federal government's dirty little secret is that Native American tribes are not fully sovereign nations in today's society as many people are led to believe. My comments made at the roundtable last Friday were about this reality and current laws that govern the relationship between tribes and the federal government."[6]

Beside the fact that Gosar was on the one hand implicating himself in the maintenance of a "dirty little secret" and on the other hand appearing to denounce it, he was referring obliquely to another concept in federal Indian law known as the "plenary power doctrine." First articulated in 1886 in *United States v. Kagama*, most scholars agree, and then more explicitly in *Lone Wolf v. Hitchcock* (1903), the plenary power doctrine ostensibly holds that Congress has unlimited authority to unilaterally make decisions about Indian lands and rights. It has no constitutional basis and was, like the other doctrines that emerged from the Marshall Trilogy, an invention of the Supreme Court.

According to Native legal experts Wilkins and Lomawaima there are three ways that the plenary power doctrine can be (and has been) interpreted:

1. Plenary power as an *exclusive power* of Congress, meaning that the Constitution recognizes Congress alone as the sole authority among the three branches of government to "regulate commerce with foreign nations . . . states . . . and with the Indian tribes" (one of only two places in the Constitution that mentions Indians).
2. Plenary power as *preemptive power*; Congress has power that preempts and supersedes the authority of states.
3. Plenary power as *unlimited and absolute* power. [All emphases in the original][7]

The first two interpretations are seen as constitutionally supported, while plenary power as unlimited and absolute power is not, even though it has been widely deployed in this way by the Supreme Court throughout the twentieth century. Wilkins and Lomawaima, along with other scholars, argue that this interpretation of the doctrine is based on several errors in the court's analysis in *Kagama*. In the *Lone Wolf* decision, they write, Justice Edward D. White (who wrote the opinion)

> inaccurately stated that Congress had exercised plenary authority over tribal lands "from the beginning" and that such power was "political" and therefore not subject to judicial review. These statements were legal rationalizations, yet they were in line with the reigning view that federal lawmakers held of Indians—Indians were dependent wards subject to their sovereign guardian, the United States.[8]

Wilkins and Lomawaima further contend that plenary power interpreted as unlimited and absolute is "aberrant and undemocratic." Laurence Hauptman (quoting Alvin J. Ziontz) likewise argues that it "is an extraordinary doctrine for a democracy to espouse."[9]

The trust doctrine—another bedrock principle in federal Indian law—is also a vexed concept upon which legal scholars disagree. Like the plenary power doctrine, the trust doctrine has been subject to a wide range of interpretations and meanings, and there is no consensus on when the doctrine originated. Some believe that it originated in the "'discovery era' of Europe's commercial and religious excursions into the Americas," others believe it was an outgrowth of the Indian law cases of the 1820s and 1830s, and still others think it was a fiction of the American Indian Policy Review Commission of the mid-1970s.[10] There is also wide disagreement on what exactly "trust" means. In an "antitrust" view, Congress can exercise unlimited and absolute plenary power over the management of Indian affairs, or what can be thought of as a theory of non-beneficial trust. On the other hand, others believe that the trust doctrine—commonly referred to as the "trust responsibility"—obligates Congress to manage Indian affairs in a way that benefits them, and that they even have a fiduciary responsibility to Indian nations. In other words, Indians are not wards of the state but are trustees in a trust relationship. In this definition, the United States is morally obligated and is accountable for violations of the trust relationship.[11]

Paul Gosar's "wards of the government" comment was highly inflammatory and viewed as a race-baiting tactic. Aside from the fact that it was factually inaccurate, it was an overt display of congressional hostility toward Native nations. It reflects a skewed and very conservative view of both the plenary power and trust doctrines, for which there are not absolute definitions as he would have us believe. It is a prime example of how these highly controversial concepts can be used to justify political agendas that not only work against Native peoples, but also, in this case, against the good of the general public.

"SPORTS MASCOTS HONOR NATIVE AMERICANS"

At an Atlanta Braves baseball game, fifty thousand fans are whipped into a frenzy, many of them dressed in Halloween-costume-style feathered headbands, their faces unself-consciously painted in "war paint," doing the "tomahawk chop" to a contrived Indian drumbeat. The same thing happens at Kansas City Chiefs football games. The Cleveland Indians flaunt Chief Wahoo, a cartoon Indian that was likened to a "red Sambo" by Cleveland councilman Zack Reed.[1] In Dallas, a gay pride parade annually features a float called "Kaliente" with a banner that reads "Honoring Native Americans." The float and accompanying marchers are dressed in all manner of Halloween-style Indian garb, and the float is a mishmash of pseudo-Indian symbols ranging from totem poles to a life-size papier-mâché buffalo. At music festivals like Coachella, Sasquatch, and Bamboozle, where fashion matters as much as music, Native headdresses have become all the rage. These are only a handful of countless examples of Native American cultural appropriation that can be named, a phenomenon that is so complex and persistent that the topic has filled volumes. Because of the vast scope of the issue, we devote the next two chapters to the most egregious and common aspects of it.

Sociologist James O. Young writes that cultural appropriation happens when people from outside a particular culture take elements of another culture in a way that is objectionable to that group.[2] According to Young's definition, it is the objection that constitutes appropriation, as distinguished from cultural borrowing or exchange where there is no "moral baggage" attached. Native American cultural appropriation can be thought of as a broad range of behaviors, carried out by non-Natives, that mimic Indian cultures. Typically they are based on deeply held stereotypes, with no basis at all in knowledge of real Native cultures. This acting out of stereotypes is commonly referred to as "playing Indian," and, as Philip Deloria's research so eloquently revealed, it has a long history, going at least as far back as the Boston Tea Party.[3] Some forms of appropriation have been outlawed, as is the case with the Indian Arts and Crafts Act of 1990 (IACA). Responding to the proliferation of faux Indian art (which undermines economic opportunities for actual Native American artists), the IACA is a truth-in-advertising law that regulates what can legitimately be sold as Indian art. No such possibility exists, however, for the vast majority of appropriations American Indians endure daily.

Non-Native people play Indian whenever they don any garb that attempts to replicate Native culture (however serious or trivial their intent) or otherwise mimic what they imagine to be Indian behavior, such as the tomahawk chop, a fake Indian dance, or bogus war whoop.[4] Native American appropriation is so ubiquitous in US society that it is completely normalized, not only rendering it invisible when it occurs, but also adding insult to injury. Native people are also shamed for being "hypersensitive" when they protest. Halloween costumes, popular fashion, and children's clubs and activities (such as the YMCA's Indian Guides and Princesses programs and other summer camps) are some of the more obvious ways cultural appropriation occurs through Indian play in mainstream society, but perhaps its most visible form is in school and sports team mascots. Campaigns to

put an end to the turning of American Indians into mascots began in the early 1960s when the National Indian Youth Council
began organizing on college campuses to remove Indian sports
stereotypes.[5] Then in 1968 the National Congress of American
Indians (NCAI), the largest pan-Native representational and
advocacy organization in the United States, established its own
anti-mascot initiative.[6] Once obscure, the movement to eradicate Indian mascots has snowballed into mainstream awareness.

In 2013 the NCAI issued a report outlining their position on
Indian mascots. It mentions numerous resolutions that have
been passed by the organization over the years, including one
in 1993 imploring the Washington professional football team
referred to as the "Redsk*ns" to drop its name, and another in
2005 supporting the National Collegiate Athletic Association
(NCAA) ban on native mascots, nicknames, and imagery.[7]

The report summarizes the negative impacts that Indian
mascots have been shown to have on Native youths, citing,
for example, a study by cultural and social psychology scholar
Stephanie Fryberg. Her 2004 study revealed that when exposed
to stereotypical "Indian" images, the self-esteem of Native
youths is harmed, eroding their self-confidence and damaging
their sense of identity.[8] This is crucial given that the suicide rate
among young American Indians is epidemic at 18 percent, more
than twice the rate of non-Hispanic white youth, and contex-
tualized by the fact that Native Americans experience the highest rates of violent crimes at the hands of people from another
race.[9] Since the early 1970s thousands of public and postsecond-
ary schools have dropped their Indian mascots, and hundreds
more professional and governmental institutions have adopted
resolutions and policies opposing the use of Native imagery and
names, including the American Psychological Association, the
American Sociological Association, the National Association

for the Advancement of Colored People (NAACP), and the US Commission on Civil Rights. In 2015 California became the first state to ban "Redsk*ns" as a mascot name in public schools. As the NCAI report indicates, the "Redsk*ns" name is particularly offensive to Native peoples. According to the report,

The term originates from a time when Native people were actively hunted and killed for bounties, and their skins were used as proof of Indian kill. Bounties were issued by European companies, colonies, and some states, most notably California. By the turn of the 20th century it had evolved to become a term meant to disparage and denote inferiority and savagery in American culture. By 1932, the word had been a term of commodification and the commentary on the color of a body part. It was not then and is not now an honorific. . . . The term has since evolved to take on further derogatory meanings. Specifically, in the 20th century [it] became a widely used derogatory term to negatively characterize Native characters in the media and popular culture, such as films and on television.[10]

Over the last twenty-five years, at least twenty-eight high schools have abandoned the name, but the Washington football team's owner, Dan Snyder, has stalwartly insisted that he will never change the name, despite mounting legal challenges to its trademark and public outspokenness by President Barack Obama and other political leaders about its offensiveness.[11] A growing number of media outlets and prominent sports reporters have vowed to stop using the name, and even NFL commissioner Roger Goodell has acknowledged its insensitivity.

Although arguments to justify the usage of Native images in the world of professional sports are weak at best, there are some instances where the use of Native mascots has been deemed acceptable at the college level, according to the NCAI report. The NCAA ban, for instance, includes a "namesake exception" that allows universities to keep their Native American nicknames and logos when they are based on a specific tribe and they have been granted the permission by that tribe. Such permission was granted for Florida State University ("Seminoles"), Central Michigan University ("Chippewas"), and the University of Utah ("Utes"). The University of North Dakota, on the other hand, due to opposition of the name "Fighting Sioux" from local tribes, was not granted an exemption. At the high school level, at least one high school in New York State has successfully fought to retain its Native mascot despite a request from the state's education commissioner to boards of education and school superintendents to end their use of American Indian mascots and team names. Salamanca Central High School (SCHS) is located within the boundaries of the Seneca Nation, 26 percent of its student body is American Indian, and the team name "Warriors" is represented by an accurate depiction of a Seneca sachem rather than the cartoonish Plains-style Indian so typical of Native mascots. A name change was opposed by the Seneca Nation of Indians Tribal Council, the SCHS administration and student body, the Salamanca school board, and the Salamanca city council in a show of cross-cultural solidarity.[12]

Native cultural appropriation via fashion is nothing new. It has been around at least since the counterculture of the 1960s and 1970s. Pop icon Cher did her part when she appeared on national television dripping with silver and turquoise Navajo jewelry and singing about Cherokee "half-breeds." The same was true for an entire generation of alienated middle-class white youth who, adorned in beads and feathers, were moving into teepees on hippie communes. Things got so convoluted that when Sacheen Littlefeather went in front of the country to reject an Academy Award on behalf of Marlon Brando in 1973, dressed in full traditional regalia, she was accused of not being a real Indian and of renting her dress. So when a new generation began parading around in Native "war bonnets" and other Indian-inspired attire at music festivals and on fashion runways and magazine covers, it was simply business as usual—only there was a new generation of American Indians and their allies, who were well-informed, mobilized, and unwilling to sit idly by and take it without vociferous criticism and even lawsuits.

Designer Paul Frank, for example, drew outrage from the Native American community in 2012 when he threw a high-profile, star-studded, Indian-themed bash (called "Dream Catchin' Powwow"), complete with plastic tomahawks, bows and arrows, war paint, and feathers. Getting the message loud and clear, the company issued an apology and announced a series of positive steps that included plans for a new collection by Native American designers, with proceeds to be donated to a Native organization.[13] That same year the Navajo Nation filed a lawsuit (which it eventually won) against Urban Outfitters for trademark violations after the company used the word "Navajo" for underwear and flasks.[14] And in 2014—as if completely oblivious to what was happening in the fashion world—hip-hop artist and fashion designer Pharrell Williams appeared on the cover of *Elle UK* magazine in a costume version of a Plains-style feather headdress, for which he later apologized.[15] Even some mainstream US Americans understood the transgression when *Time* magazine published an online opinion piece spelling out just why the image was so odious. Pointing out that clothing designers are notorious for borrowing from other cultures for inspiration, and comparing fashion to cultural fusion in cooking, the author wrote, "The link between clothing and personal identity, however, means that putting on another culture's clothes is a greater claim to ownership and belonging than sampling sushi or buying a burrito for lunch. As long as nudity isn't a socially acceptable option, we are what we wear—and our desire to define ourselves through borrowed finery can either enrich or impoverish the source community."[16]

Among other things, it is this subtle claim to ownership that scholars of cultural appropriation unmask, especially in the realm of mascot names and images. With university and college examples like the Florida State Seminoles, the University of Illinois Fighting Illini, and many others, non-Native mascot defenders claim such representations honor particular tribal nations and peoples. But what they really do is assert an imagined indigeneity whereby white dominant society assumes control of the meaning of Nativeness. Professor of professional sport management at Drexel University Ellen Staurowsky characterizes these kinds of fraudulent claims to Indianness as a system of sustainable racism within a "sociopolitical power structure that renders Indianness tolerable to Whites as long as it is represented on terms acceptable to them."[17] She also points out the inconsistency of tolerating objectionable university Indian mascots with the central mission of higher education.

The myth that Indian mascots honor Native Americans, then, appears to be little more than a carefully constructed rationale to justify the maintenance of a system of domination and control—whether intentionally or unintentionally—where white supremacy is safeguarded, what Robert F. Berkhofer Jr. famously called the "White Man's Indian." And particularly at the level of professional sports, the branding of Native American team names and images also serves more as a rationale to maintain financial empires (explaining the stubborn adherence to racist portrayals of Native peoples in organizations like the Washington Redsk*ns), than dubious claims to be honoring them. But the justifications for American Indian cultural appropriation don't end with sports team mascot battles and fashion debacles. Appropriating Native cultures by playing Indian permeates US society so broadly it strikes at the very heart of Native American cultures, their spiritually based systems of belonging and identity, which we turn to next.

"NATIVE AMERICAN CULTURE BELONGS TO ALL AMERICANS"

James Arthur Ray was at the top of his game in 2009. He'd fashioned himself into a celebrity self-help guru, becoming a darling of the television talk show circuit with appearances on *Oprah*, *The Ellen DeGeneres Show*, *Larry King Live*, and frequently *Today*. He had rocketed to fame after being a featured subject of a 2006 book and companion movie, both called *The Secret*, which provided a road map to personal empowerment and wealth. By 2008 he was a *New York Times* best-selling author with *Harmonic Wealth: The Secret of Attracting the Life You Want*, his third book. Not surprisingly, Ray's expertise didn't come cheap—his individual mentorship could cost upwards of $90,000, and the price tag for a week-long "Spiritual Warrior" retreat in Sedona, Arizona, was almost $10,000.[1] In October of that year, however, Ray's New Age self-help empire came crashing down when three people were killed in a sweat lodge ceremony he conducted and eighteen others were hospitalized with injuries ranging from burns to kidney failure.

A sweat lodge ceremony is an ancient spiritual tradition among many Indigenous peoples that is still widely practiced today. It is a purification ritual performed inside a small lodge, where water poured on fire-heated rocks creates a cleansing steam. Ray was convicted of negligent homicide, served two years in prison for the crime, and was ordered to pay $57,000 in restitution to the victims' families. After his release the conditions of his parole, curiously, did not bar him from conducting self-help seminars or sweat lodges.[2]

Indian country responded with fury, and Native media pundits pointed out all the ways Ray had gone wrong. He had violated all the protocols that Native spiritual leaders carefully adhere to, including grossly incorrect construction of the lodge, the use of improper herbs and other substances, and not allowing breaks to cool the lodge (known as "rounds").[3] Navajo journalist Valerie Taliman called it "a bastardized version of a sacred ceremony."[4] According to American Indian traditions, only spiritual leaders with many years of training are allowed to conduct sweat lodge ceremonies, and it is often a right that is inherited through family or other kinship lineages. James Ray had no such lineage or training. Many in Indian country voiced outrage that Ray received only a two-year sentence for the deaths caused by his charlatanism. And if all of that were not bad enough, Ray's sweat lodge victims had paid obscene amounts of money to participate in a sacred ceremony that Indian people say should never involve money.

James Ray's cultural appropriation was hardly an isolated incident. By 1993 the appropriation of Native spirituality had become so widespread that a gathering of Lakota, Dakota, and Nakota people drew an international audience of some five hundred people to pass a "'Declaration of War Against Exploiters of Lakota Spirituality,' denouncing individuals involved in the New Age movement, shamanism, cultists, and neo-paganists and others who promote 'intolerable and obscene imitations of sacred Lakota rites.'"[5] Ten years later—with apparently no perceivable improvement of the situation—a proclamation was issued by Arvol Looking Horse, the Nineteenth Generation Keeper of the Sacred Calf Pipe, prohibiting non-Native participation in Lakota ceremonies. As Suzanne Owen writes, "The reasons why the Lakota Declaration and the Looking Horse Proclamation are significant documents in the debates about appropriation are due to the prominence of Lakota models in representations of Native American spirituality."[6] Not that the Lakota are the only ones whose ceremonies and culture are being appropriated. As Owen notes, the proposed prohibitions, according to Lakota and other Native American activists, are as much to protect the well-being of practitioners as the integrity of Native ceremonies. Ceremonial protocol not followed correctly can be dangerous, they warn.[7]

In their endeavors to understand how and why playing Indian manifests as spiritual appropriation, scholars have offered various analyses, all of which share several common traits. One is the recognition of non-Natives' sense of entitlement to practice Native American cultures and religions. This entitlement is expressed implicitly as claims to Native heritage—the mythical idea that Native American heritage equals US heritage—that what belongs to Native people should be shared by all. Explicitly, it comes out as a stated right.

Rayna Green first articulated the concept of playing Indian in a 1988 essay where she argued that the phenomenon likely originates from the captivity experiences of Europeans. Transforming eventually into cultural performances that relied upon the removal and death of real Indians, playing Indian at its core reflected an inherent hatred of Indians, not love or affinity.[8] From the Boston Tea Party forward, US Americans obsessed on vanishing Indians in a multitude of ways that translated into trying to *become* them, or at least using them to project new images of themselves as they settled into North America and left Europe behind. The historical practice of white people becoming Indian is visible in the social and civic clubs where versions of Indianness were (and in some cases still are) enacted, including Tammany Hall (aka the Society of St. Tammany, the Sons of St. Tammany, and the Colombian Order), the Elks, the Lions, the Kiwanis, the Improved Order of Red Men, the YMCA's Indian Guides and Princesses program, and the Boy Scouts of America

Koshare Dancers. Even Indians were conscripted into playing Indian, with performances like the Wild West Shows of the late nineteenth century, and the projections of Indianness became ubiquitous (and literal) with the development of photographic and cinematographic technology. By the 1960s, young white Americans were transforming themselves into pseudo-Indians and showing up in droves on Indian reservations, looking for a way of life different from the consumer-oriented Christian conformity of their parents. Indian images—however imaginary and distorted—have so infiltrated US American consciousness that they appear in consumer products in everything from butter packaging to recreational vehicles. Business names like Navajo Express (trucking), Mohawk Industries (floor coverings), and Apache Software can be seen. From Rayna Green's perspective, each era of US history exhibited some form of Indian play. The spiritual appropriation of the New Age movement is thus only one recent manifestation of it.

By the 1980s, the hippie counterculture had evolved into the New Age movement. Lisa Aldred wrote in 2000 that this was a consumerist movement, and that while not all New Agers flock to Native American spiritual practices, "a small percentage constructs their essential identity around Native American religion." Aldred contended that the biggest business for Indigenous appropriation was in book publishing, where "plastic medicine" authors were big sellers.[9] Among the more familiar of them are Carlos Castaneda, with his many best-selling books on the sorcerer Don Juan Matus; Lynn Andrews, who became known as the "Beverly Hills Shaman"; Mary Summer Rain, who purported to record the teachings and prophecies of a blind Indian medicine woman she calls No Eyes; and Brooke Medicine Eagle, with her generic version of "Native American wisdom" drawn from various specific traditions.[10] Echoing Green, Aldred asserted that New Agers were far more interested in exotic images and romanticized rituals built on distorted stereotypes of Native peoples than they were in the sociopolitical realities of Native peoples living under conditions of colonialism. This put them in adversarial positions when Native people objected to what they perceived as cultural theft. Based on ethnographic fieldwork and other research, Aldred found that

> the most frequent defense New Agers made to Native Americans' objections against misappropriation of indigenous traditions was couched in First Amendment terms. New Agers consistently argued that their right to religious freedom gave them the "right" to Native American religion. . . . The commercialization of Native American spirituality in both books and products also suggests that consumers "own" Native American spirituality in some sense.[11]

Among New Agers' defenses against charges of appropriating American Indian spirituality, Aldred also found claims that spirituality and truth cannot be owned, and that "spiritual knowledge belongs to all humans equally."[12] Aside from the contradiction that the consumerist aspect of the New Age movement inevitably entails claims to ownership via products and copyrights, it also implies the universality of "truth." In this case, it is a claim that all spiritual knowledge held by Indigenous peoples is universally true across the great divide of cultural difference.[13]

Viewing the issue as based in a First Amendment right bespeaks the very different paradigms that frame dominant white society and that of American Indians. For US Americans the discourse about rights is undergirded by the rugged individualism enshrined in the Constitution and Bill of Rights and a fundamental belief in universalism. Religion is thought to be a matter of personal choice and is ultimately disconnected from culture. The freedom of religion, then, is a matter of the rights of individuals and part of the right to pursue happiness. For American Indians, however, spirituality is part of a broader cultural context where religion is not separate from culture. As part of the continuum of culture, an Indigenous nation's spirituality is a reflection of the circumstances of life connected to specific places over vast expanses of time and in the context of particular worldviews and language. The origin stories, language, and worldviews of a people—and thus their spirituality—are what Native people call their "original instructions." Those original instructions are oriented toward the survival of the people and the perpetuation of their cultures more than they are toward any promises of personal happiness or individual enlightenment (although it could be said that these are natural effects of strong, healthy cultures), and they are certainly not thought to be meant for everybody universally.[14] In short, the frame of reference non-Native people bring to their practice of American Indian spirituality is wholly different—and arguably inconsistent with—those of Indian people.

Playing Indian vis-à-vis explicit and implicit claims to ownership of Indigenous culture has ramifications beyond the issues of mascots and spiritual appropriation. One of the more recent stereotypes of Native American people to emerge since the counterculture, for example, is the image of the ecological (or environmental) Indian as it was famously depicted by Iron Eyes Cody, the "crying Indian" of the early 1970's anti-littering campaign.[15] This newest form of the Noble Savage stereotype, while not an overtly antagonistic view of Indians, still upholds Native peoples as primitive and prescribes a vision of them as projected through a white lens. It is most problematic in environmental discourses where nature and humans are perceived as separate from each other, often pitting non-Native concepts about environmentalism against Native goals for use of land

and resources, which are part of larger sovereignty struggles. Shepard Krech III writes, in *The Ecological Indian*,

> The connections between Indians and nature have been so tightly drawn over five hundred years, and especially in the last quarter of the twentieth century, that many non-Indians expect indigenous people to walk softly in their moccasins as conservationists and even (in Muir's sense) preservationists. When they have not, they have at times eagerly been condemned, accused of not acting as Indians should, and held to standards that they and their accusers have seldom met.[16]

Finally, one of the most controversial forms of playing Indian occurs at the level of personal identity claims, especially where prestigious professional positions and other material benefits are at stake. Often referred to as ethnic fraud, dubious claims to Indian identity are muddled in abstract rhetoric about the complexity wrought by colonialism or the personal right to claim an identity by choice. History is plagued with examples of non-Indigenous people passing themselves off as Indian for personal gain. In one of the more famous twentieth-century cases, the Englishman Archie Belaney pursued a successful literary career under the alias Grey Owl. Traveling the lecture circuit during the 1920s and 1930s in North America and Europe sporting full buckskins and headdress, Belaney kept his fraudulent identity a secret until after his death.[17]

By the second half of the twentieth century, impostors were abundant, most often masquerading among the literary ranks of the New Agers. But in the 1990s a more ambiguous identity claim emerged among the Indigenous intelligentsia in academia with Ward Churchill, perhaps best known for publishing a controversial article on the heels of the 9/11 World Trade Center attacks. Churchill's claim to Cherokee and Creek heritage—upon which he'd based much of his reputation as a Native American scholar—appeared to have been unsubstantiated, while an investigation finding academic misconduct resulted in his firing from the University of Colorado Boulder. A few years later, in 2008, noted scholar Andrea Smith came under fire when genealogical searches turned up nothing to substantiate her claims to Cherokee lineage. A petition for tenure was subsequently denied at the University of Michigan.[18] The Smith issue would reemerge in 2015 with a social media campaign created anonymously to discredit her after it was discovered that Rachel Dolezal had falsely claimed African American heritage, prompting her resignation as president of the Spokane, Washington, chapter of the NAACP. In 2012 senatorial candidate Elizabeth Warren was publicly lambasted for claiming Cherokee and/or Delaware heritage on her application to Harvard Law School. And in 2015 another controversy erupted when Dartmouth's Native American Program announced the hiring of Susan Taffe Reed as its new director. Reed is a member of a group called the Eastern Delaware Nation, which is viewed as an illegitimate Indian tribe since it has no official state or federal recognition. Genealogical searches on Reed's heritage also turned up no documented Native ancestry. All of these cases are examples of what Native scholars call "box-checking Indians," people who claim Native heritage in the context of college and universities (which strive to increase their diversity), knowing that they will not be asked to produce documentation to back up their claims.[19]

Some forms of Native American cultural appropriation are clearly more egregious than others. In terms of personal identity claims, the need for documentation is troubled by the fact that American Indians are the only US citizens who are required to document their ethnicity in order to meet legal definitions, a reality scholars often connect to the eliminative impulse of the settler state. There is undoubtedly a sizable population of people who legitimately descend from Indigenous peoples who will never be able to prove it for a multitude of reasons resulting from federal policies designed to assimilate Indigenous peoples or otherwise eliminate them. But in the case of broader socio-logical phenomenon like mascots and New Age posers, non-Native people playing Indian says as much about non-Native US Americans' unsure collective sense of themselves as it does about their ambivalence toward American Indians. As Philip Deloria suggests, it offers the opportunity to experience a contrived sense of "aboriginal Americanness"[20] in the face of its de facto absence, simultaneously building a foundation for and reflecting the mythological belief that Native American culture is by default everyone's culture.

Playing Indian overall can also be thought of as "a move to settler innocence," based on the hard-hitting essay on decolonization by Eve Tuck and K. Wayne Yang. In this framework settler innocence is the investment in maintaining the settler structure to avoid actual, material decolonization, where the restoral of Indigenous lands and sovereignty is the objective: "strategies or positionings that attempt to relieve the settler of feelings of guilt or responsibility without giving up land or power or privilege, without having to change much at all. In fact, settler scholars may gain professional kudos or a boost in their reputations for being so sensitive or self-aware. Yet settler moves to innocence are hollow, they only serve the settler."[21]

Tuck and Yang hold that ultimately decolonization must ensure the future existence of Indigenous peoples and not concern itself with guaranteeing a settler future; they argue for an "ethic of incommensurability," meaning that although not all questions are immediately answerable, they will be revealed in time. They also acknowledge what may be perceived as an "unfriendly" delinking of coalition politics in order to achieve a decolonized future for Indigenous peoples.[22]

"MOST INDIANS ARE ON GOVERNMENT WELFARE"

One of the most common myths about Native Americans is that they receive a host of "free" benefits just for being Indian or that they don't pay taxes, all amounting to an enduring belief that Indians are permanently on the dole. Many American Indians have been asked by non-Native people at least once in their lifetime if they receive a monthly check from the government. Non-Native people go on genealogical quests to find an Indian ancestor in the hopes of obtaining a free college education and other "benefits" for their children. Others resent what they perceive as undue favoritism. When it comes to politics, political leaders employ antagonistic language about the unconstitutionality of "race-based" criteria when it comes to determining policies favorable to Indigenous peoples, and political campaigns have been won and lost based on rhetoric about Indians "not paying their fair share." At the core of all these scenarios is a fundamental lack of understanding about the nature of the relationship between Native nations and the US government.

It is true that Native Americans receive limited health care through the Indian Health Service (IHS), part of the Department of Health and Human Services, which is responsible for providing those services to members of American Indian and Alaska Native nations. According to the IHS website, "The provision of health services to members of federally recognized tribes grew out of the special government-to-government relationship between the federal government and Indian tribes.

This relationship, established in 1787, is based on Article I, Section 8 of the Constitution, and has been given form and substance by numerous treaties, laws, Supreme Court decisions, and Executive Orders."[1]

An IHS fact sheet goes on to refer to its mission as a legal obligation under federal law. It emphasizes the trust relationship, with its basis in the treaties the United States signed with hundreds of Native nations, which "frequently call for the provision of medical services, the services of physicians, or the provision of hospitals for the care of Indian people," in partial exchange for the land they ceded to the United States.[2] Because the treaties exist in perpetuity, so do the obligations contained in them. The Snyder Act of 1921 authorizes Congress to appropriate funds for the Indian Health Service, and the Patient Protection and Affordable Care Act of 2010 (so-called Obamacare) created permanent reauthorization of the Indian Health Care Improvement Act. While Native Americans can receive services at Indian hospitals and clinics throughout the United States, the Indian Health Service has been plagued by chronic underfunding, increasingly so in recent decades. For example, in 2014 IHS reported that it spent $2,849 per capita annually on its user population, compared to federal health-care spending on the whole population, which was $7,713 per person.[3] The result is only the most basic of services where they do exist and an absence of services altogether in many places.

When it comes to higher education only a very few Native people have access to tuition-free four-year degrees. Tribal colleges and universities (TCUs) are schools that are established on or near Indian reservations and are run by tribes. There are thirty-four TCUs in the United States, and two other colleges—Haskell Indian Nations University and Southwestern Indian Polytechnic Institute—are run by the federal government under the Bureau of Indian Education (BIE).[4] The TCUs are funded by scholarships students receive through the American Indian College Fund, which also provides scholarships to non-TCU schools. In general, qualification for admission to the BIE schools requires membership in a federally recognized tribe or the ability to document one-quarter or more Indian blood degree, or both. To qualify for scholarships at the TCUs, one must be able to document membership in a federally recognized tribe or be a descendant of an enrolled member. While the TCU scholarship requirements are less restrictive, the scholarships are highly competitive and not guaranteed, and the same is true for other federal and private scholarship programs.[5] Some tribes offer partial scholarships for their tribal members but they rarely if ever cover all tuition.

TAXES

In 2003 Arnold Schwarzenegger was elected governor of California thanks to an aggressive and high-profile campaign in which he characterized Native nations with casinos as "special interests" that were "not paying their fair share." The message was clear: Indians are being given a special ride, because they don't pay taxes. It didn't seem to matter that the allegations were patently false.[6]

Federal law recognizes the governmental nature of Indian nations in the US Constitution, and as sovereign governments, tribal nations are not subject to certain forms of taxation since sovereign governments do not tax each other—a fact that led to the perpetuation of the myth that Indians don't pay taxes. However, in the case of Indian gaming, revenue and taxes are indirectly generated at the federal, state, and local levels. According to a National Indian Gaming Association report,

In 2013, Indian gaming generated over $13.6 billion for federal, state and local government budgets through compact and service agreements, indirect payment of employment, income, sales and other state taxes, and reduced general welfare payments.

In addition, individual Indians pay federal income taxes, the people who work at casinos pay taxes, and those who do business with tribal casinos pay taxes.

Finally, tribal governments also made more than $100 million in charitable contributions to other tribes, nearby state and local governments, and non-profits and private organizations. Through these contributions, Indian gaming revenues saved thousands of jobs for American healthcare workers, firefighters, police officers, and many other local officials that provide essential services through the recession.[7]

While Indian nations' tribal gaming enterprises are not subject to federal income tax, income derived from gaming and distributed in per capita payments to individuals is taxed.[8]

Despite laws that preclude the taxation of revenues generated from Indian trust lands, the Internal Revenue Service for years aggressively attempted to collect taxes from them, leading to a crisis that came to a head in 2012, culminating in congressional hearings in June and September that year. In one account from the June hearing, harassment and intimidation tactics against the Oglala Sioux at Pine Ridge in South Dakota included IRS agents showing up unannounced and demanding records for everything from powwow prize money and funeral monies to health-care and education benefits. Protesting the harassment as a violation of treaty rights, one tribal member recounted being told by the IRS agent, "You can read your treaties in prison, if you like."[9] At the September hearing three tribal leaders testified that the IRS was moving to tax non-gaming per capita payments held in BIA trust accounts, in violation of the Per Capita Tax Act of 1983.[10] From a tribal government perspective, the taxing of non-gaming monies paid to tribal citizens through certain programs (such as funeral funds and health and education benefits) should have been illegal under the IRS's General Welfare Doctrine, also known as the General Welfare Exclusion (GWE) rule. The GWE rule was originally intended to apply to state benefits paid to citizens. However, as an Advisory Committee on Tax Exempt and Government Entities report asserted, guidance for the applicability of the GWE to tribal citizens under particular tribal benefit programs was unclear.[11] Addressing the need for clarity under the GWE, Indian country leaders mobilized to remedy the situation by advocating for a legislative fix.[12] This was drafted in both the House and Senate as the Tribal General Welfare Exclusion Act of 2013, which was easily passed in 2014.[13]

Also responding to the taxation crisis, the Center for World Indigenous Studies, based in Olympia, Washington, conducted its own preliminary study on taxation in Indian country. Titled *Federal Funding to Indian Nations and Communities Tax Payments to the United States: A Preliminary Assessment*, the brief study not only addressed the GWE problem but raised other more troubling issues as well. First of all, it found that overall American Indians and Alaska Natives paid almost as much money in taxes as they received from the federal government in the form of grants and contract revenues—revenues directly connected to the federal government's treaty responsibilities. Of the $8.4 billion Native nations receive annually (based on 2012 figures), $8.1 billion ultimately leaves the communities to pay taxes at the local, state, and federal levels. The net effect, the study suggests, is that tribal governments are paying the United States to live up to its treaty obligations, and the shortfalls created by perpetual underfunding means that tribes must meet the deficits themselves by relying on profits generated from tribal businesses to provide services to their citizens. The study notes that while revenues derived from trust resources are not taxed, since 1924, when citizenship was unilaterally extended to Indians, the IRS has increasingly sought to impose taxes on tribal businesses and personal income.[14]

The preliminary findings of the study concluded that

> what growth has occurred in Indian economic activity has been mainly due to Indian nations acting in their own self-interest and not due to infusions of U.S. federal funds in the form of grants and contracts. Indeed, funds expended for the benefit of American Indians and for Indian Affairs by the Federal government peaked in the mid-1970s and has fallen in real current dollar values since.[15]

LEGAL SETTLEMENTS

Indigenous nations have for many decades negotiated with and litigated against the United States for its unfair and many times illegal dealings with them, dealings that have resulted in the massive loss of land and resources. Beginning with the Indian Claims Commission in the 1940s, the United States has paid out billions of dollars in settlements in acknowledgment of its depredations, with Native nations sometimes extinguishing their right to aboriginal title or status as federally recognized tribes in exchange.[16]

The largest settlements have occurred in recent years, the most significant of them being the Claims Resolution Act of 2010, signed into law by President Obama after more than fifteen years of litigation in the Cobell case. The Cobell lawsuit contended that the federal government as the trustee over Indian lands had for over a century mismanaged the accounts of individual Indians (called IIM accounts) for lands that were leased out for various income-producing activities like timber harvesting, cattle grazing, or mining. The court acknowledged that the accounting was so bad (practically non-existent) that it would never be possible to accurately account for how much money had not been paid to individual Indians under those leases. After years of negotiations, a $3.4 billion settlement amount was reached, nearly arbitrarily. The settlement was divided into three segments that allocated money to tribal governments to consolidate fractionated interests on reservation lands, payments to individual Indians, and to fund higher education scholarships.

In a separate but related lawsuit referred to as the "Settlement Proposal to the Obama Administration" (SPOA) in 2012, forty-one tribal governments settled with the federal government after twenty-two months of negotiations for alleged mismanagement of trust assets. The $1 billion settlement was said to "fairly and honorably resolve historical grievances over the accounting and management of tribal trust funds, trust lands and other non-monetary trust resources that, for far too long, have been a source of conflict between Indian tribes and the United States," according to Attorney General Eric Holder.[17]

Another large settlement—$940 million—was reached in 2015 after Supreme Court justices ruled in favor of hundreds of Native nation governments. The court affirmed that the Interior Department had failed to cover contract costs for services it was obligated to provide under federal law, such as health care and housing. Under the settlement some tribes would receive as little as eight thousand dollars while others would be entitled to much larger amounts, as is the case with the Navajo Nation, which could receive as much as $58 million.[18]

The legal settlements are the result of centuries of US dishonor and misdeeds and Native nations pursuing justice in courts of law, not because of a sense of benevolence originating from the federal government. Despite the settlements and other services provided under the federal government's trust responsibility, Indigenous people as a group consistently top the lists of socioeconomic indicators for poverty, ahead of other non-Native ethnic groups and whites. In 2014 the Pew Research Organization published an article claiming that one in four Native Americans still lives in poverty and that Native Americans are plagued by extremely high levels of unemployment and lower levels of educational attainment than non-Natives.[19]

"INDIAN CASINOS MAKE THEM ALL RICH"

As may be apparent by now, the stereotypes that so stubbornly depict Indigenous people in the US media and history books play out in many ways and have no inherent logic. A perfect example is how Native people can simultaneously be represented as collectively all on government welfare and rich because of casinos. Despite the inherent contradiction, these stereotypes are often deployed for nefarious political agendas, such as when Arnold Schwarzenegger characterized Indians as "special interests" who were "not paying their fair share." The tactic in this case was to convince California voters that Indians are merely special interest groups (as opposed to sovereign nations) and that they are all wealthy, ostensibly because of gaming. Implied in this rhetoric is that because they were not paying their fair share, they were not just being given a free ride but actually somehow cheating the system. If we deconstruct this implied meaning, we open a Pandora's box full of familiar old tropes that have been reworked and given new life. We will return to this, but first let's examine the facts about Indian gaming in general.

According to data gathered by the National Indian Gaming Commission in 2014, there were 459 gaming establishments in Indian country. (There are currently 567 federally recognized tribal nations, but because some tribes have more than one casino, this number does not mean that 459 tribes have casinos.) In 2014, these casinos generated $28 billion in total. A total of 295 casinos generated more than $10 million, with 96 generating between $10 million and $25 million. The other 164 casinos generated less than $10 million (and 88 of these generated less than $3 million).[1] At the top end, twenty-six casinos earned more than $250 million each. These numbers were not significantly different from 2010, when the casinos' overall revenues were $26 billion. The Harvard Project on American Indian Economic Development reported in 2007 that Indian gaming revenues grew rapidly between the mid-1990s and 2004, from $5 billion in annual revenues to $19 billion.[2] Their report stated:

> Despite growing vigorously, Indian gaming has not grown evenly. There are substantial disparities in facilities' sizes and success. . . . The median casino facility brought in $4.9 million in 1995 net income, and the profits transferred to tribes [were] less than $20 million for more than 80% of the tribes observed. . . . More recent National Indian Gaming Commission figures show that the Indian gaming sector has continued to demonstrate wide variation. . . . Out of the 367 tribal facilities in operation in 2004, the 15 largest accounted for more than 37% of total Indian gaming revenues, and the 55 largest tribal facilities accounted for close to 70% of total sector revenues. Concomitantly, many tribes' gaming operations were relatively small, located in remote areas with low populations. 94 facilities had annual revenues of less than $3 million in 2004, and the smallest 219 operations (60% of the 367 facilities nationwide) accounted for only 8% of total Indian gaming revenues.[3]

More recently, reports show that growth has plateaued since 2007. In a 2014 US Senate Committee on Indian Affairs hearing on gaming, the Department of the Interior assistant secretary for Indian affairs, Kevin Washburn, testified that "the days of tremendous growth are probably behind us for Indian gaming."[4]

Growing competition within regions and from commercial casinos were given as reasons. While Ernie Stevens, chairman of the National Indian Gaming Association, was hesitant to agree with Washburn's assessment, A. T. Stafne, chairman of the Assiniboine and Sioux Nations on the Fort Peck reservation in rural Montana, said, "I will be blunt. We have seen little economic benefit from Indian gaming over the last 25 years."[5]

It is true that gaming has generally improved economic conditions in Indian country, and for a few nations, fabulous wealth has been attained. Some of that wealth does trickle down to less fortunate Indians through revenue sharing via the Indian Gaming Regulatory Act. However, gaming overall has been far from the golden goose that many (like Schwarzenegger) have made it out to be. The few reservations that exist close to densely populated areas have enjoyed the most success, while for some reservations in rural areas, casinos have helped build social infrastructure like community centers and health-care facilities, but for others still, gaming provides little more than needed jobs for tribal members. These factors can help explain the Pew Research Center's 2014 findings that one in four American Indians and Alaska Natives still live in poverty.[6] Yet despite these stark realities, the stereotype of rich casino Indians misleads the general public and keeps them perpetually misinformed.

As we asserted in our discussion about playing Indian (myth 14), the misconceptions about Native people in dominant white society always say more about white society itself than they do about Native peoples. Celeste Lacroix, a communications professor at the College of Charleston in South Carolina, agrees. Lacroix undertook a detailed examination of the casino Indian trope and the way it plays out in television depictions. She studied six popular shows, including *The Sopranos*, *Saturday Night Live*, *Chappelle's Show*, *Family Guy*, *Drawn Together*, and *South Park*, all of which had episodes that centered on images of Indians and casinos from the late 1990s through the early 2000s. She discovered that "these depictions reference age old racist stereotypes of the Ignoble Savage while simultaneously working to construct a new trope." She calls the new trope "the casino Indian." The casino Indian "resurrects and resuscitates some of the oldest and most deeply embedded significations of Native Americans and Native America," which include specifically the "dangerous savage" and the "degraded Indian." Ultimately these images are familiar portrayals of Indians as a threat to white America, but rather than Indians being a military threat to white settlement as they once were, the threat is now economic and political. Even though the portrayals are couched in humor and are meant to be satirical—which, as Lacroix acknowledges, can be effective social commentary—these depictions, she argues, position the audience to laugh at the Native characters "in an unreflexive way since the depiction does not seem to be an ironic commentary on dominant racism against Natives. Rather, it seems here to merely reinforce old tropes and introduce some new, equally disturbing images."[7]

Seeing Indians as an economic threat is actually not new, according to Alexandra Harmon in her book *Rich Indians: Native People and the Problem of Wealth in American History*. Harmon looks at seven examples of Indian wealth throughout history to understand how "reactions to Indian wealth have reflected and affected ideologies of race and nationality as well as economic ideologies. By examining controversies about affluent Indians in successive periods, we can see the changing interplay of those ideologies, other sociocultural motivations, and material conditions. We can also learn why controversy has swirled around enterprising Indians long after Indians acceded to capitalism's hegemony."[8]

Relative to gaming, Harmon noticed that "moral judgments about economic behavior merged with ideas about Indians," and "normative generalizations about Indian propensities—often paired with contrasting characterizations of non-Indians—were common."[9] Among those normative generalizations is a belief that in order for Indians to be authentically Indian they need to be poor and helpless.

Native studies scholars Jeff Corntassel and Richard C. Witmer II characterize white anxiety about Indian wealth as "rich Indian racism." In their book *Forced Federalism: Contemporary Challenges to Indigenous Nationhood*, the authors illustrate how rich Indian racism has negatively influenced state and local policymakers, resulting in the undermining of Indigenous nations' authority to be self-determining. A prime example is Arnold Schwarzenegger's gubernatorial campaign and his deployment of the rich casino Indian trope to garner votes. Other examples are cited as well, where lawmakers have exercised their power to extort and illegally tax gaming nations based on the social construction of rich Indians who are perceived to have "special rights."[10] Corntassel and Witmer reiterated the on-the-ground facts of Indian gaming as of 2008 when their book was published, putting the economics into perspective:

> The 43 largest casinos, which represent only 5.5 percent of the overall reservation population, generated 64 percent of the total gaming revenues ($10.7 billion) in 2004. In contrast, the 10 lowest-earning casinos, representing 42 percent of the overall reservation population, earned just 1 percent of all casino revenue. . . . Furthermore, according to a 1998 Native Americans in Philanthropy study, even if gaming revenues were distributed equally to all indigenous peoples in the United States, the amount distributed, $3000 per person, would not be enough to raise the indigenous per capita income of $4500 to the current U.S. average of $14,400.[11]

In the hypothetical scenario described, even if we accounted for the increased revenues recorded, ten years later the numbers don't appear to be enough to raise the per capita income to average US levels. Yet the rich casino Indian stereotype persists. By 2005 it had even found its way into high school textbooks, according to Jeffrey Hawkins at the University of Memphis. Hawkins writes that when high school textbooks cover American Indians, they tend to categorize them by two broad stereotypical approaches: the "dead and buried" cultural approach, and the "tourist" approach "which allows students to visit a 'different' culture [Indians] that usually only includes the unusual (rituals, customs, etc.) or exotic (living on reservations) components of Native American culture." Surveying seven diverse secondary US history textbooks in the largest school districts in California and Tennessee, Hawkins found that the books revealed the emergence of some new stereotypes. One in particular, the depiction of Native Americans in association with casino gaming or gambling, is also accompanied by misleading illustrations or text (or both) that portray all Indians as "either living on a reservation or connected to reservations in some form," despite the fact that at that time the majority of Indians (65 percent) were not living on reservations.[12]

"INDIANS ARE
ANTI-SCIENCE"

Few people in the world have more reason to be anti-science than American Indians, given the history of the way science was used in service of US political agendas to dispossess them of their lands and subjugate them. It was a point alluded to in 2012 by Jason Antrosio, a professor of anthropology at Hartwick College, in a blog on an anthropology website.[1] Specifically, Antrosio expressed his understanding about why many Native Americans refuse to participate in genetic studies. He was responding to a post on another anthropology blog in which the author, writing under the pseudonym Dienekes Pontikos, claimed that the "big hole" in genetic sampling of Native groups in the United States is due to "petty identity politics contra science."[2] Echoing this, a commentator at the *Discover* magazine blog wrote that "Native Americans are not special snowflakes" (because they are not the only ones who have been subject to historic injustices) and that "holding a grudge is no excuse for anti-science."[3] The arrogant condescension of these and other science writers reflects a belief that Indigenous Americans somehow owe their DNA to genetics studies and that when they disagree, they are automatically deemed to be against science.

While experience has taught Native Americans that there are very good reasons to be leery of genetic testing, flippant statements about being anti-science are at best unfair and at worst not just incorrect, but also inflammatory and provocative.[4] These statements are irresponsible and only build obstacles

between Native peoples and Western-based science communities, and genetic science is only the most recent realm to exhibit such anti-Indian antagonism. There is an abundance of
evidence embedded in Native cultures—and scholarship to back
it up—that is the opposite of these vitriolic claims, highlighting
the fact that Native people have always had their own forms of
science and modes of knowledge production, even if they aren't
recognized as such by positivist, Cartesian-based Western
systems. One of the biggest challenges for Indigenous people
in North America (and elsewhere) is being seen by dominant
populations as peoples with legitimate systems of knowledge,
a problem thanks to centuries of white supremacy that constructed Indigenous peoples as inferior in every way. As one
of the preeminent scholars on Native science, Gregory Cajete,
points out, elders, activists, scholars, and intellectuals have told
a different story.[5] The word "science" as it is commonly used
refers narrowly to complex, specialized, and mechanistic systems of measurement to understand what we call reality. Literally translated, however, science refers simply to systematized
knowledge. In this sense, all Native peoples have their own
structures of empirically based knowledge. From their observa-
tions they developed technologies that made their lives easier,
in characteristically sustainable ways. The following are five of
the most ancient, well known, and influential of those Indigenous technologies.

ASTRONOMY

Astronomy is one of the oldest forms of science. Consistent
with Native worldviews that recognized the interdependence of
all life, even the stars and other celestial bodies were seen as
relatives who guided the lives of the people in tangible ways.
The movement of celestial bodies could determine ceremonial cycles and festivals, or war and other events of political or

religious significance. They also figure prominently in the creation stories of many peoples. Like peoples all over the world, Indigenous peoples read the heavens to keep track of time. Calendar systems like Plains peoples' winter count and other forms of pictographs, drawings, and rock art (such as those found throughout the American Southwest and the painted caves of the Chumash) were records that allowed people to maintain important traditions year after year. Some, like the Nazca geoglyphs in Peru, are thought to possibly be manifestations of geometry and mathematics. One of the most pragmatic applications of astronomical knowledge was its ability to guide cycles of planting and harvesting.

HYDRAULIC ENGINEERING

Many Indigenous cultures in pre-contact North and South America were known to have complex irrigation systems that could sustain communities of thousands of people. Archaeological evidence from the Hohokam culture (ancestors of the Tohono O'odham people in today's Arizona) and Peruvians in pre-Incan and Incan times suggests irrigation technology that includes canals, pipelines, aqueducts, dams, reservoirs, and check valves dating back to 300 BC, far earlier than European technological advances.

AGRICULTURE

Contrary to the popular colonial myth of Indians as nomadic wanderers, many (if not most) Native nations were agriculturalists of the highest degree. What we today call "permaculture" is, as Cajete wrote, "in reality applied Indigenous science."[6] Indigenous knowledge of bioregional sustainability sometimes even included game management. Great Lakes peoples cultivated rice, cattails, and pond lilies.[7] All over North and South America, Indigenous peoples experimented with farming techniques, resulting in many of the world's most widely consumed food crops today. For example, Iroquois and other Native North Americans planted the Three Sisters—corn, beans, and squash—together to ensure long-term soil fertility and maximum output. Growing these crops in small mounds prevented soil erosion compared to linear plowing, and the technique was adopted by some European immigrant farmers. Furthermore, Native peoples practiced hybridization techniques long before researchers like Gregor Mendel and Luther Burbank popularized them, resulting in many varieties of corn, chilies, beans, and squash. And the so-called Mississippian Mound Builders in the US South, the predecessors to today's Cherokee, Choctaw, and other Southeast peoples, have long been the subject of archaeological and anthropological study in complex pre-Columbian civilizations. Cahokia, located in today's Illinois, is exemplary. A city at the time larger than London, it is thought to have supported a population of between twenty thousand and fifty thousand people at its height in around 1250 to 1300 because of the ability to produce surplus food.[8]

TRANSPORTATION AND ROAD BUILDING

In North America after the last ice age, Native peoples had no use for the wheel because species that might have been draft animals had gone extinct. But Native Americans were highly mobile and constructed a network of trails that are still evident today. What became pioneer wagon trails such as the Santa Fe and Oregon Trails, the Central and Southern Overland Trails, the Wilderness Road (through the Cumberland Gap), and the Natchez Trace are still visible on maps as highways.

In Mexico, the Mayans built a network of roads centered in the Yucatán city of Cobá around AD 623. These roads were remarkable for their rubble-filled raised construction that ranged from two to eight feet above ground and were lined with limestone concrete. Roads were as long as sixty-two miles, and archaeologists have found a five-ton cylindrical roller for packing the ground, similar to steamroller equipment used today.[9]

In South America, the Incas constructed a twenty-four-thousand-mile complex of roads centered around the city of Cuzco, roads that extended as far away as the Amazon and Argentina.[10] These included suspension bridges, solid bridges with stone piers and wooden decking, and even tunnels cut through solid granite. Bridges crossed gorges, marshes, and other seasonally wet areas and incorporated culverts to prevent water from flooding them.

WATER NAVIGATION AND VESSELS

Wherever there was water, Indigenous peoples developed watercraft. In North America, canoes were common among coastal, lake, and river populations. Great Lakes peoples built bark-covered canoes, and Arctic peoples constructed sealskin kayaks. Pacific Northwest peoples constructed elaborate dugout canoes big enough to hold as many as twenty people and thousands of pounds of cargo, and their maritime history is among the oldest in the world. The Chumash and Tongva peoples of coastal Southern California were known for their *tomol*, a sewn-plank canoe that is considered one of the oldest forms of seafaring craft in North America.[11] It is believed by some scholars to be influenced by ancient Polynesians.[12] Recent discoveries on Santa Rosa Island off the coast of Southern California confirm the ancient ocean-navigating abilities of the Chumash people dating back at least eleven thousand years, far predating the seafaring cultures of ancient Egypt, Europe, and Asia.[13]

As is true for peoples globally, the technological innovations of ancient Indigenous peoples were grounded in particular worldviews. They were formed by their experiences within specific places over millennia. Scholarship from Indigenous peoples everywhere emphasizes that there are different ways of knowing the world, beyond the dominant educational paradigms that privilege Eurocentric philosophical foundations. These foundations can be traced to (among other things) Judeo-Christian traditions that construct and continually reinforce social hierarchies and views through a lens of domination and alienation from the natural world.[14] Indigenous knowledge construction broadly speaking, on the other hand, rests in a view of the world grounded in relational thinking, respect, and reciprocity, which translates as a sense of responsibility to life in all its many and diverse forms. Scholars actively assert these differences within contemporary academic discourses—even within the hard sciences—through associations, curriculums, and educational approaches that reflect these values.

Take as an example the American Indian Science and Engineering Society (AISES). Founded in 1977, the group sees no inherent conflict between American Indian values and those embodied in the sciences. Quite the opposite, in fact, says Cherokee engineer and educator George Thomas:

I feel [science] is actually a natural thing for Native Americans because of our relationship to the Earth, our spiritual beliefs, and respect for The Creator's great laws. Science is really just a way of understanding what The Creator has put here. It's not just an academic pursuit for us; science and theology are one and the same. It is also a mistake to assume that technology is exclusive to one culture or another. Take for example the teepee. It's a very aerodynamic shape that can withstand high winds and snow loading, with strong convection heating and cooling properties.[15]

According to the AISES mission statement, the group sustains 186 chartered college and university chapters, 14 professional chapters, and 170 affiliated K–12 schools supporting American Indian students in the disciplines of science, technology, engineering, and math (STEM). Similarly, the Society for Advancement of Chicanos/Hispanics and Native Americans in Science (SACNAS) is a collaboration dedicated to supporting the educational success of Hispanic and Native American people in science.

Native American perspectives have woven themselves into college-level education throughout the United States as evidenced by the Native American Science Curriculum. The curriculum engages Indigenous research methods that are applicable in tribal contexts such as resource management, while also working to break down derogatory stereotypes and biases.[16] And innovative projects at the K–12 level are infusing Indigenous traditional environmental knowledge (TEK) into conventional Western-based environmental education. With a multimillion-dollar grant from the National Science Foundation in 2010, for instance, the Indigenous Education Institute partnered with the Oregon Museum of Science and Industry to create a traveling exhibit called *Generations of Knowledge* that blends TEK with Western science, showcasing "culturally relevant contexts as valuable, complementary ways of knowing, understanding and caring for the world."[17]

"INDIANS ARE NATURALLY PREDISPOSED TO ALCOHOLISM"

Few images of Native peoples have been as intractable and damaging as the trope of the drunken Indian. It has been used to insidiously and overtly support the claims of Indian inferiority that, as we have seen, have been deployed in a host of ways that result in loss of culture, land, and sovereignty. The trope is deeply woven into US social narratives—perpetuated both in popular culture and in scholarly circles—and it plays out in a number of ways. For instance, the drunken Indian male (a version of the degraded Indian) is often seen as morally deficient because of his inability to control himself, making him a menace to society. Or he has become alcoholic because of his tragic inability to adjust to the modern world—he is the Indian stuck between two worlds, and he is pitied. More recent explanations of Indian alcoholism hold that it is genetically inherited. Regardless of the prevailing stereotype, the underlying logic is that Indians are somehow predisposed to addictive drinking, more so than non-Native people, who, naturally, can "hold their liquor."

Europeans introduced alcohol to American Indians as an instrument of trade and diplomacy. By the time the Great Plains were being settled by Europeans, virtually all treaty negotiations included complex and subtle uses of alcohol, and alcohol even became a bargaining chip.[1] But it is well known that Indians were no strangers to consciousness-altering practices. Plants such as datura, peyote, and tobacco were widely used in questing for visions and spiritual knowledge. Don Coyhis and William White noted that some Southwestern tribes used not only psychoactive plants ceremonially, but also ritualistically used alcohol made from fermented plants long before European contact.[2] Some have observed that Native forms of alcohol were weak compared to the Europeans' distilled spirits.[3] They further point out that white settlers and military personnel on the frontiers were notorious for their extreme drinking. Indians would have learned and emulated the extreme social drinking of whites and had little time to develop their own rules and protocols for socially acceptable alcohol consumption.[4] But because Indians were commonly viewed as inferior to begin with, Indian antisocial drunken behavior was particularly demonized, and as John Frank, Roland Moore, and Genevieve Ames suggest, historical written accounts about Indian drinking must be seen in this light.[5] Although abstinence by entire tribal groups was not uncommon, tribal and colonial authorities attempted bans on alcohol trade in Indian territories, which were largely ineffective in groups that did drink. Also ineffective was legislation outlawing the sale of alcohol to Indians, a law first passed by Congress in 1832 and not repealed until 1953.[6]

Studies on American Indian drinking behavior didn't begin surfacing until the second half of the twentieth century. Conventional wisdom held that Native contact with alcohol led to "instant personal and cultural devastation," but a landmark study in 1969 by MacAndrew and Edgerton and subsequent studies began challenging those beliefs.[7] In a 1971 study, anthropologist Nancy Oestreich Lurie hypothesized that drinking at some point became a way for Indians to validate and assert their Indianness in the face of negative stereotypes such as the disappearing Native. Lurie argued that Indian drinking was "the world's longest ongoing protest demonstration."[8] Similarly, Frank, Moore, and Ames argued that the influence of alcohol resulted in a culture of drinking in Indian country, character-ized as group-oriented and uncontrolled, among other things.[9] These studies frequently emphasized the sociohistorical roles alcohol has played in Indian drinking.

Understanding Indian alcohol use in the context of colo-nial history works to deconstruct the stereotypes that stigma-tize Indians as predisposed to alcoholism compared to other populations. The myth about Native American predisposition to alcoholism is accompanied by numerous other related mis-conceptions about Native Americans and alcohol, as the work of Phillip A. May has shown. Not only do the misconceptions spring from bigoted historical tropes. They also, as May sug-gests, stem from flawed research and misconstrued results.[10] The most controversial is the biological determinist position that alcoholism is genetic. May argues that this is based solely on one study that reported that Indians metabolize alcohol more slowly than non-Indians, a study that was later criticized as highly flawed. As May writes, "Major reviews of alcohol me-tabolism among all ethnic groups usually conclude that alcohol metabolism and alcohol genetics are traits of individuals and that there is more variation within an ethnic group than there is between ethnic groups. Further, when biophysiologic investi-gators attempt to explain major alcohol-related behaviors, they generally point to sociocultural variables as the major factors."[11]

Since May's 1994 study on the epidemiology of American In-dian alcohol use (in which he refutes the idea of genetic inheri-tance), no research has conclusively confirmed the theory. It's true that research has exposed deeply troubling statistics regard-ing alcohol use in Indian country, but as May wrote, the common myths and misunderstandings stem from gross oversimplifica-tions.[12] Researchers do seek to understand things like the dis-proportionately high rates of alcohol-related deaths among the American Indian population. An oft-cited study by the Indian

Health Service in the mid-1980s, for instance, determined that on average, Indians die more frequently of alcohol-related causes than non-Indians. Indian deaths in alcohol-related car and other accidents were found to be three to four times higher than non-Natives; Indian suicide was found to be one and a half to two times higher; Indian deaths due to homicide were found to be roughly two times higher; and Indian deaths due to alcoholism were found to be five and a half to seven and a half times higher. These realities can be explained, May says, in three ways. First, the differences can be accounted for by demographic, social, and political differences experienced by American Indians. Demographically, the American Indian population is relatively young (in 1988 the median age was 32.3), and younger populations overall tend to have much higher rates of alcohol-related death. Sociopolitical considerations such as low socioeconomic status also exacerbate alcohol-related problems. Second, American Indian drinking styles tend to be more flamboyant, characterized by abusive drinking (such as binge drinking) and high blood alcohol levels. Third, the mixing of alcohol impairment with risky behaviors and risky environments further contributes to higher mortality rates. Most Indian people still live in rural Western states where higher death rates can also be expected due to higher-risk environments, greater distances from care facilities, and lack of availability of services.

It should be emphasized that while we can think of many of these factors as behavioral, none of them automatically indicate defined patterns of addictive drinking. As May argues, there is a distinction to be made between alcohol abuse and alcoholism. Furthermore, even in light of the alarming statistics on alcohol-related death in Indian country, it would be inaccurate to say that alcoholism is the leading cause of death among American Indians. Another factor May analyzes has to do with the prevalence of drinking among American Indians, that is, how pervasive problem drinking is throughout Indian country. Despite the stereotypical understanding that the vast majority of Native American people drink, the facts are quite different. May clarified that there were few extant prevalence studies, but certain facts stand out from the few that do exist. First of all, prevalence varies widely from tribe to tribe. In some groups prevalence is lower than the US general averages, while in others it is about the same or higher. The studies also indicate that these averages can and do change over time, either becoming higher or lower. And while findings confirm that among Native American adults who do drink, there is a substantially higher prevalence of problem and excessive drinking than among the whole US population, more positive findings conclude that among American Indian males who are middle-aged and older, more completely quit drinking than among most other groups of US males, and in virtually every tribal group a lower proportion of women drink. May stresses, "The overall prevalence of drinking among Indians is not the most important variable in the epidemiology of drinking. What is more important are the drinking styles, some of which emphasize very problematic behaviors."[13]

There is another crucial line of analysis scholars take when studying alcohol use in Indian country that questions the context from which most research emerges. In their groundbreaking book *Native American Postcolonial Psychology*, Duran and Duran draw from critical social sciences scholarship and point out that the medicalization of alcoholism and alcohol-related problems presents certain other conceptual problems in how the phenomenon is framed.[14] In their view, alcoholism and alcohol abuse are social problems, and medicalizing them means that standards of an ideal and presumably neutral subject are created, against which all others are measured.[15] The flaw is that those standards are inevitably based on the norms of a middle-class dominant white culture. "The focus of research has too often been the individual and his/her maladaptive adjustments to life in the late twentieth century," they write.[16] In this model the Native problem drinker or alcoholic is seen as pathological when his or her alcohol abuse is determined to stem from an inability to adjust to mainstream society. In this framework Native cultural inferiority is once again reinforced. For Duran and Duran this logic extends beyond alcohol-related problems and more broadly into mental health care in the Indian community. They write that

> in addition to alcohol-related problems, many of the well-intentioned researchers find deviance and powerlessness in their investigations of Indian life-styles and subjectivity. In addition, these findings, as in the case of the Indian alcoholic, conversely construct an objective norm—the approximation of which measures health. The problem for native peoples is that this norm looks surprisingly like an idealized European American cultural life-style and worldview.

They also point out that when some of these well-intentioned researchers posit a lack of socialization into either Indian or Western culture, they fall prey "to a static view of culture and disavow the changing contingent nature of postmodern society" and risk problematically constructing a monolithic pan-Indian person who lacks the specificity of a tribal identity.[17] In other words, it is a mistake to lump all Indian people together as a single group when applying theories of alcohol abuse in Indian country.

From Duran and Duran's perspective, the topic of alcohol-related behavior in Indian country is too frequently viewed outside of historical context, allowing definitions that mask the issues of domination and subjugation. They even go so far as to say that "what is not recognized is that alcohol use and even suicide may be functional behavior adaptations within a hostile and hopeless social context."[18] As morbid as it might sound, their point is that these responses can be seen as rational—as opposed to pathological—behavior, given the historical circumstances. It also opens the space to acknowledge the role in alcohol abuse of historical trauma, a subject that is gaining greater attention in mental health care within Indian country.[19] Likewise the roles of historical loss and discrimination ought to be considered relative to alcohol abuse.[20] Duran and Duran advocate for a "postcolonial histor[y] of alcohol" that situates a discussion of alcohol-related problems within a colonial discourse and recognizes the long history of culturally based responses to alcohol abuse within Indian nations.[21] To summarize, the myth about American Indian predisposition to alcoholism is as false as saying that white people are naturally predisposed to alcoholism. To even suggest that Indians are simply more prone to alcohol abuse than non-Natives implicitly makes assumptions about the superiority of the dominant white society and thus the inferiority of Native peoples. It ignores a complex array of variables that must be considered in assessing alcohol abuse in Indian country.

"What's the Problem with Thinking of Indian Women as Princesses or Squaws?"[1]

It is essential to acknowledge the diversity among Indigenous women in the United States. They are citizens of hundreds of distinctive Native nations that have particular cultural practices, languages, and precolonial histories, as well as experiences under US colonialism. Some live in reduced portions of their nations' original territories on reservations, some live on reservations to which their ancestors were moved (most of the Indigenous peoples from east of the Mississippi were forcibly removed to Indian Territory, now Oklahoma), and many live in cities (about half of the Native population lives and works in urban areas). As Choctaw scholar Devon Abbott Mihesuah writes: "There is no one voice among Natives because there is no such thing as the culturally and racially monolithic Native woman."[2] And there never has been.

That is exactly the problem. Although the stereotypes have changed over time, they are nearly always monolithic, as if Native Americans are a racial or ethnic group. Centuries of British and US domination of Native nations produced the binary of the "Indian princess" and the "squaw," which purports to describe both Native women's bodies and their status. The counterparts for male Natives are the romanticized "warrior" and the degraded "savage."

Of course, Pocahontas was the first "Indian princess," and that mythologized figure persists in Disney films and other

Hollywood movies. Conjured by many Euro-American women as an original ancestor, Pocahontas is always portrayed as beautiful and depicted as having lighter skin and being more European looking than other Native people and a having a petite but shapely body. This sometimes borders on child pornography, given that the historical Pocahontas was a child when she met John Smith.

The mythical "Indian princess" is a common stereotype. Sacajawea and other Native women scouts, albeit not categorized as "princess," are portrayed as compliant and helpful to US government spies, such as Lewis and Clark, and to fur traders and explorers. Often Indian princesses are portrayed as daughters of tribal chiefs. Scholars have stated that the myth of Pocahontas helps to perpetuate white Eurocentric values because she leaves her tribe and becomes a Christian, and this insinuates that Christianity is better than traditional Indigenous religion. Thus, the myth of Pocahontas becomes a method of promoting Eurocentric values and norms and a tool of colonialism.[3]

On the other side of the binary, the usage of "squaw" has fallen into disrepute with the rise of multiculturalism, but it is still ubiquitous in Hollywood westerns as well as historical documents. There are also still around a thousand official place names in the United States in which the term is used.[4] Further, it remains an active stereotype of traditional Native women even when the term itself is not used. In literature, movies, and histories we see images of a drudge, a sort of beast of burden, a very dark, silent figure who is doing all the heavy lifting in Indigenous settings, with the males either engaged in warfare or lazing around while women do the work or follow a distance behind the men.

Both the Indian princess and the squaw constitute racist stereotypes of Indigenous women meant to render whites superior and help perpetuate white patriarchal European values. The precolonial roles and status of women varied among the hundreds of societies of North America, depending on whether the particular nation was agriculturally based (the majority), reliant on seafaring and fishing, transhumant, or harvesters of wild rice, acorns, berries, nuts, and other wild foods. The roles of Haudenosaunee, Cherokee, and Muskogee women of the eastern half of North America into Canada, women of the Pueblo and Hopi city-states, and Navajo women in what is now the US Southwest have been much researched and found to be remarkable when compared with women's roles in western Europe on the eve of Columbus's infamous appearance in the Americas. In these agricultural societies, women were the creators of seeds and hybrids, and they planted the crops. Men participated in tending and harvesting. Each of these nations had divergent forms of governance, but their economic bases in food production (corn, beans, and squash of many varieties and colors) were similar, as were their communal social relations. Pueblo women were also the architects and builders, while men were stonecutters and weavers. These were matrilineal societies in which women controlled directly or ceremonially the equitable distribution of land use and food.

Women's roles in governance varied but were probably strongest among the Haudenosaunee (the federation of the Mohawk, Oneida, Onondaga, Cayuga, Seneca, and Tuscarora nations). Certain female lineages controlled the choice of male representatives for their clans in governing councils. Men were the representatives, but the women who chose them had the right to speak in the council, and when the chosen male representative was too young or inexperienced to be effective, one of the women might participate in council on his behalf. Haudenosaunee clan mothers held the power to recall unsatisfactory representatives. Charles C. Mann, author of *1491: New Revelations of the Americas Before Columbus*, calls this governance structure "a feminist dream."[5]

That dream of freedom, solidarity, and equity that was the lodestone of precolonial North America was trampled on by Spanish, French, and British explorers, gold seekers, and oppressive colonial regimes, but only the British had developed the institutions of settler-colonialism before planting colonies in North America. They had developed these methods and practices in the conquest and subjugation of the Irish, pushing small farmers off their lands to be replaced by commercially oriented settlers, both Anglo and Scots. British fencing of the commons to develop capitalistic sheep production and textile mills deprived communities of the wood, streams, and wildlife they depended on. A large, disgruntled, landless, and jobless population was persuaded to take the arduous one-way journey to British outposts on the Atlantic Coast of North America. This then was the start of British colonialism in North America, then New Zealand and Australia: exporting their surplus people, including convicts, with promises of land and wealth if they could wrest it from the deeply rooted Indigenous civilizations already there. They brought with them the patriarchal culture developed under Roman and Christian laws and practices, a level of subordination of women unknown in North America but inherent to the culture of conquest and settlement, which was based on violence and violation of Native women.

Indigenous women have continued to bear the brunt of colonial violence, specifically sexual violence, both within families and by settler predators, and, increasingly, sex traffickers. Incidence of rape on reservations has long been astronomical. The colonialist US restrictions on Indigenous policing authority on reservations—yet another legacy of the doctrine of discovery and the impairment of Indigenous sovereignty—opens the door to perpetrators of sexual violence who know there will be no consequences for their actions.[6] Under the US colonial system, jurisdiction for crimes committed on Native lands falls to federal authorities, because Native justice can be applied only to reservation residents, and then only for misdemeanors.

One in three Native American women has been raped or experienced attempted rape, and the rate of sexual assault on Native American women is more than twice the national average. For five years after publication of a scathing 2007 report by Amnesty International, Native American and women's organizations, including the National Organization for Women (NOW), lobbied Congress to add a new section to the 1994 Violence Against Women Act (VAWA) addressing the special situation of Native American women living on reservations.[7] The added provision would give Native nations' courts the jurisdiction to arrest and prosecute non-Native men who enter reservations and commit rape. At the end of 2012, the Republican-dominated US Congress denied reauthorization of the VAWA because it included the provision. In March 2013, however, that opposition was overcome, and President Barack Obama signed the amended act back into law, although it has limited effect.

Another difficulty for Indigenous people in general in the United States, but especially for the women, Lenape scholar Joanne Barker points out, is the demand for demonstrable Native authenticity—which really means to appear and act in a particular prescribed manner. This demand on women within Indigenous communities is not only emotionally painful but also creates social inequalities and injustices associated with the US patriarchal order of racism, sexism, homophobia, and fundamentalism. Barker sees that overcoming internal colonization is critical to achieving decolonization and self-determination. Native women scholars like Barker are in the forefront of exposing these issues and seeking resolutions.[8]

In her book *Indigenous American Women: Decolonization, Empowerment, Activism*, Devon Abbott Mihesuah describes and analyzes the various ways that many non-Indigenous and some

Indigenous men and women, even sophisticated academics, view Native women. In so doing, she exposes the damages wrought by colonialism and male supremacy as they limit the full involvement of Native women in higher education and prevent them from realizing traditional Indigenous roles. Centuries of imposed colonialism and Christianity also manifest in patriarchal practices within Native communities, changing the relations between women and men, with the resulting sexual violence outlined above. Other results that Mihesuah points to are severe income gaps and internal factionalism, which fall heaviest on women and families, producing self-degradation when women are not able to carry out their traditional responsibilities. However, Mihesuah finds positive changes that Indigenous women are making in their lives, relationships, and professional advancement. This is in part rooted in the key role that Native women have played in the past forty years of resurgent Native resistance.

This resurgence arose after the 1953 congressional resolution to terminate the treaty-based legal existence of all Native nations, an attempt to carry out a bloodless genocide to complete the violent genocidal US Army and settler militia campaigns of the nineteenth century. Termination was to proceed accompanied by a vigorous relocation program. Younger Natives would voluntarily abandon reservations and relocate to designated urban areas, with some initial expenses paid. This, the US ruling class believed, would make forced dispersal unnecessary. Immediately Native people began to organize, and some looked into possible redress through the United Nations.[9]

In 1961 young relocated Natives, along with some who had not left the reservations, formed themselves into the intertribal National Indian Youth Council (NIYC), based in Albuquerque, with Mohawk intellectual Shirley Hill Witt playing a central role in building the organization nationally and Navajo artist Gloria

Emerson doing so in the Southwest.[10] At the same time, workshops were organized that brought together equal numbers of young Native women and men. In 1964, NIYC organized support for the ongoing Native movement to protect treaty-guaranteed fishing rights of the Swinomish, Nisqually, Yakama, Puyallup, Stilaguamish, and other Indigenous peoples of the Pacific Northwest, in which the leadership included the extraordinary Ramona Bennett and Janet McCloud.

While local actions multiplied in Native communities and nations during the 1960s, the spectacular November 1969 seizure and following eighteen-month occupation of Alcatraz Island in San Francisco Bay grabbed wide media attention. Native American students and community members living in the Bay Area initiated an alliance known as Indians of All Tribes. They built a thriving village on the island that drew Native pilgrimages from all over the continent, radicalizing thousands, especially Native youth. Indigenous women leaders were particularly impressive, among them LaNada (Means) War Jack, Madonna (Gilbert) Thunderhawk, Reyna Ramirez, Aileen Cottier, and many others who have continued organizing and serving as role models into the twenty-first century.

Three years later, in 1973, hundreds of militarized FBI and other federal and state agencies surrounded Wounded Knee, a hamlet on the Lakota Pine Ridge reservation in South Dakota, and so began a two-and-a-half-month siege against the American Indian Movement (AIM) protesters at the 1890 massacre site. Wounded Knee was made up of little more than a trading post, a Catholic church, and the mass grave of the hundreds of Lakotas slaughtered by the US Seventh Cavalry in 1890. During the 1973 siege, armed personnel carriers, Huey helicopters, and military snipers surrounded the site, while supply teams of mostly Lakota women made their way through the military lines and back out again through dark of night. Again, as at Alcatraz,

Lakota leader Madonna Thunderhawk was prominent, as were dozens of other women of all ages, both inside and outside the besieged compound, who organized support systems around the country.

As important as women organizers and activists to reconstructing Indigenous cultures and governance are the several generations of Native women scholars, writers, and poets (who themselves are also community activists). Seneca scholar Mishuana Goeman observes of them: "Rather than stand on the periphery, Native women are at the center of how our nations, both tribal and nontribal, have been imagined."[11]

"NATIVE AMERICANS CAN'T AGREE ON WHAT TO BE CALLED"

In 1992 Oprah Winfrey, in her daytime talk show, ran a series on racism. One of the episodes dealt with racism against Native Americans and featured a panel of American Indians and non-Indians. In a conversation about racist terms and names (such as "squaw" and "Injun") Oprah posed the question, "Do you want to be called Native Americans, or American Indians, or—?" One of the panelists, Suzan Shown Harjo, responded with a chuckle, "All terms are wrong, so use them interchangeably."[1] Oprah then asked, "And why are all terms wrong?"—to which Harjo replied, "They are Eurocentric and racist." Visibly flustered, Oprah joked that she didn't know what to say, leading to the obvious question from an audience member, "What do you call yourself?" Harjo replied that it's most accurate to call Indians by their specific national names. Trying to sum it up cohesively, Harjo said, "Call us whatever you want; just don't call us names."

The conversation galvanized several issues at once but highlighted the fact that referring to Indigenous peoples by catchall phrases like "Native American," "American Indian," or simply "Indian" is problematic, and for many reasons there is no one correct term. We can fairly speculate about what Harjo meant when she said the terms are Eurocentric and racist. The term "Indian," most scholars acknowledge, is a term that originated with Columbus in his encounters with Indigenous peoples of the Caribbean, mistakenly believing he had landed in the East Indies. It is Eurocentric because the word was a term of convenience for the interlopers who couldn't distinguish between differing cultures and languages and because it suited centuries of European newcomers rather than respecting the nations' words for themselves. The same is true for the term "American Indian," but qualifying the term "Indian" with "American" adds another layer of imposition by inferring the centrality of US ("American") legal dominion, a concept many Native people today still find highly offensive. "Native American" is a term that arose after the civil rights movement in response to a need for unbiased terminology regarding historically maligned ethnic groups. While perhaps a step in the right direction, it still highlights a relationship of historic domination. The Eurocentrism inherent in all of the terms defines the racism at the root of them all, especially given that the terms are imposed by outsiders in Native peoples' own homelands. As legal scholar Peter d'Errico wrote, "'American Indians' derives from the colonizers' world-view and is therefore not the real name of anyone. It is a name given to people by outsiders, not by themselves. Why should we use any name given to a people by someone other than themselves?"[2] D'Errico goes on:

> We have to discard both "American Indian" and "Native American" if we want to be faithful to reality and true to the principle that a People's name ought to come from themselves. The consequence of this is that the original inhabitants of this land are to be called by whatever names they give themselves. There are no American Indians or Native Americans. There are many different peoples, hundreds in fact, bearing such names as Wampanoag, Cherokee, Seminole, Navajo, Hopi, and so on and on through the field of names. These are the "real" names of the people.

But the conundrum of names doesn't end there. Some of the traditional or "real" names are not actually derived from the people themselves, but from their neighbors or even enemies. "Mohawk" is a Narraganset name, meaning "flesh eaters." "Sioux" is a French corruption of an Anishinabe word for "enemy." Similarly, "Apache" is a Spanish corruption of a Zuni word for "enemy," while Navajo is from the Spanish version of a Tewa word. If we want to be fully authentic in every instance, we will have to inquire into the language of each People to find the name they call themselves. It may not be surprising to find that the deepest real names are often a word for "people" or for the homeland or for some differentiating characteristic of the people as seen through their own eyes.[3]

Other terms are applied to Native people internationally, including "Aboriginal" and "First Nations," but they are more specific to particular places, in this case Australia and Canada. In the late twentieth century, the term "Indigenous" came into wide usage throughout the Americas and the international community. Meaning the condition of being original to a region or a country, the term has come into favor as a more accurate description for peoples with existences that long predate modern states and histories of colonial intrusions into already occupied territories. The term "Indigenous" reflects a sense of global solidarity among all Indigenous peoples who share common struggles against the ongoing impositions of states, situating them as international actors with specific claims to territories and rights that supersede state authority and distinguish them from domestic state populations.[4] Indigenous peoples are officially recognized in international institutions such as the International Labour Organization (beginning in the 1930s, the first to consider Indigenous issues) and the United Nations, although Indigenous peoples don't have political standing equal to states.[5] Even with the passage of the UN Declaration on the Rights of Indigenous Peoples (UNDRIP) in 2007—the most far-reaching international instrument that recognizes Indigenous self-determination to date—Indigenous peoples still have a long way to go because UNDRIP does not have the weight of an international treaty.

Some scholars have pointed out that even the term "Indigenous" is problematic. One commentator in particular, Steven Newcomb, has written extensively on the need to deconstruct the meaning of words and phrases relative to Indigenous peoples in international relations and law. Newcomb contends that a structure of state domination of Indigenous peoples is so normalized in the international arena that it fails to recognize their original freedom and independence. The state of being Indigenous is thus constituted from and defined by invasion and settlement of foreign populations. He writes:

> Then we have the working definition of the U.N. Special Rapporteur on the Problem of Discrimination against Indigenous Populations for the United Nations Sub-Commission on Prevention of Discrimination and Protection of Minorities: "Indigenous populations are composed of the existing descendants of the peoples who inhabited the present territory of a country wholly or partially at the time when persons of a different culture or ethnic origin arrived there from other part [sic] of the world, overcame them and, by conquest, settlement or other means, reduced them to a non-dominant or colonial situation. (In Sadruddin Aga Khan and Hassan bin Talal, *Indigenous Peoples: A Global Quest for Justice*, 1987)"
>
> In short, peoples termed "Indigenous" in the international arena are defined as, "Dominated Peoples" or, "Peoples under Dominance or Domination." The above words and phrases that disclose this meaning are: "overcame them"

"conquest," "settlement," "reduced them," "non-dominant," and "colonial." These are all different ways of expressing domination. The meaning is clear: Free Nations and Peoples have been *reduced down* from their original stature to an "indigenous" stature or existence.[6] [Emphasis in the original]

Overcoming the state of domination is precisely the work of Indigenous activists and scholars worldwide, and the power of naming is part of that struggle, as Newcomb's work demonstrates. In the United States, Native people are gravitating increasingly to using their traditional names, as one Indian Country Today Media Network article recently indicated. Written by Amanda Blackhorse, the article was an informal survey of a handful of prominent Native Americans of various ages who were asked what they preferred to be called. Not surprisingly, their answers ran the gamut from their tribal names to "Indian" and everything in between. The important point, as Blackhorse writes—echoing Suzan Harjo's words a generation earlier—is that "each time we choose to elect our own names and references we are empowered. This discussion does not argue that the term 'Indian' is better, or that 'Indigenous' is, or to invalidate being an American or not to be; it is about choice; what we choose as well as how and why we used these names. One thing is certain, we can all agree to reject pejorative references to Native people, e.g. 'redskins,' 'squaw,' 'savages,' etc. This discussion is complex, and I have discovered there is no singular nor [sic] simple answer."[7]

"INDIANS ARE VICTIMS AND DESERVE OUR SYMPATHY"

In the pages of this book we have discussed the myriad ways in which Indigenous peoples in the United States have endured centuries of depredations against them. These injuries are not limited to injustices of the past but are living, active processes embedded in the legal structures and social fabric of the state. In the words of Theodore Roosevelt, "The settler and pioneer have at bottom had justice on their side; this great continent could not have been kept as nothing but a game preserve for squalid savages."[1] And so it was that at the turn of the century the United States self-righteously reveled in victory achieved through profound brutality and a trail of broken and immoral laws, sanctimoniously attaching the word "justice" to the ethnic cleansing white settlers called "winning the West." American Indians had against all odds barely survived centuries of biological carnage and scorched earth policies inflicted upon them by invaders from across the Atlantic. For Indian sympathizers it would not be difficult to assign the term "victimization" to such a history, and that's just what they did. By the late nineteenth century the "plight of the Indian" had become a popular literary trope, one that endures today.[2]

The Indian plight trope arose at a time when US aggression against American Indians had reached a fevered pitch and the federal government was going to its most violent extremes to put an end to Indians' traditional lifestyles. Many openly called for extermination.[3] But in 1881 Helen Hunt Jackson's landmark book *A Century of Dishonor* indicated a turning point, with some US citizens beginning to publicly condemn the government's treatment of Indians.[4] Within a year of the book's publication the social activist group Indian Rights Association (IRA) was founded by a handful of white reformers to advocate for the full assimilation of Indian people into American life, then considered Indians' best option for survival. Considering themselves "friends of the Indian," in the long run the IRA supported policies that led to further destruction of Indian cultures and lives because of the group's failure to understand Indians' actual needs. Though seriously misguided, the IRA still signaled a newfound national conscience about Native people that led to reform movements in the twentieth century.

At the end of the nineteenth century, the American Indian population was at an all-time low, and extreme poverty plagued reservation communities as a result of white settlers' ruthless greed and moral injustices, as Jackson's book pointed out. By 1928 if anyone disbelieved the veracity of Jackson's claims, the 847-page Meriam Report (commissioned by the Institute for Government Research and funded by the Rockefeller Foundation) would dispel those doubts. The report delivered a scathing rebuke of the Dawes Act, which had been in effect for four decades.[5] The Meriam Report paved the way for a new policy objective of limited self-government, and this was legislated in the 1934 Indian Reorganization Act, also known as the Wheeler-Howard Act. What is often overlooked is that the act was passed in large measure as the result of a new generation of well-educated Native professionals organized into groups such as the Society of American Indians (SAI), founded in 1911, who were influential among white Progressive movement reformers.[6]

The SAI could be seen as the genesis of modern American Indian political activism. Even though the group seemed to align itself with the conservative objective of assimilation through the granting of citizenship (achieved in 1924), at the time the idea that Native people could be the peers of whites was a fairly radical proposition given the prevalence of racist social Darwinist ideologies. Their other overarching goal was access to the US Court of Claims.[7] Even though the group was relatively short-lived, having dissolved in 1923, its goals were eventually realized with the establishment of the Indian Claims Commission in 1946 (which monetarily settled outstanding Native land claims until 1978), and its legacy paved the way for numerous other Native professional organizations, including the National Council of American Indians and the National Congress of American Indians.[8]

Paralleling the Indian Claims Commission, new attacks on Indian country came with the termination policy of the Truman and Eisenhower years. A new kind of energy took hold in Indian country, however, aided by the building ethnic nationalist movements in the 1960s. Even the hippie counterculture would play a significant if uneasy role in Indians' newfound empowerment during the 1960s and 1970s social revolution, and Indians organized.[9] The direct action campaigns of the fish-ins in Washington State in the early 1960s, the occupation of Alcatraz Island in San Francisco, the Trail of Broken Treaties and the Bureau of Indian Affairs takeover in 1972, the Wounded Knee protests and siege in 1973, and more—all depended on the coordinated efforts of Indian activists working in tandem with broad coalitions of non-Indians to achieve renewed government commitments to uphold treaty rights, circumscribe trust responsibilities, and work overall to improve Indians' standard of living. As scholar Sherry Smith writes, "The starting point for understanding such change must be with the Native American people, tribes, and leaders who survived the termination era and continued to insist on their treaty rights, sovereignty, and cultural survival. But they knew they could not do it alone. There were simply not enough of them."[10]

The levers of power, Smith pointed out, were in non-Indian hands. By the early 1960s, a broad collection of organizations from the Left, including churches, and liberals and radical individuals of various ethnicities were lending their support to the Indian cause. "In the long term, the fundamental turn toward the spirit, if not the letter, of Hank Adams's and the Trail of Broken Treaties' Twenty Points has prevailed," Smith contends.[11]

In 1975 Richard Nixon signed into law the Indian Self-Determination and Education Assistance Act, and a plethora of strong pro-Indian legislation has followed in the decades since, including the Native American Religious Freedom Act (1978), the Indian Child Welfare Act (1978), the Indian Gaming Regulatory Act (1988), the Native American Graves Protection and Repatriation Act (1990), the Indian Energy Resources Act (1992), and the Tribal Self-Governance Act (1994).[12]

The American Indian Movement has without a doubt been the most high-profile—and controversial—of all the American Indian organizations and social movements in the twentieth century. Its militancy was attention-getting and made for good political theater but didn't always win friends and positively influence people. A 1996 study analyzing the efficacy of media messaging in the 1960s and 1970s American Indian movement, for example, revealed that instead of focusing on Indian sovereignty, treaty rights, and civil rights, AIM's raison d'être, most of the time media focused on the group's militancy, resulting in negative, off-track messaging. Not surprisingly, media coverage continued to be laden with stereotyping and tending to promote factionalism.[13] Still, further analysis supports the conclusion that while AIM's tactics were sometimes contentious and not all its demands were fulfilled, in the long run they were successful, since the group's objectives eventually became institutionalized with the federal government's policy shift toward self-determination.[14]

Even after self-determination and the government-to-government relationship with Native nations was affirmed, problems continued because the relationship was still fundamentally paternalistic, with the federal government asserting its authority over the nations like it had always done. Tribal governments were often hamstrung on their own reservation lands due to limited jurisdiction, contributing to deeply entrenched problems like violence against women and violent crimes committed by non-Natives on reservation lands. Other laws, such as the Indian Child Welfare Act (1978), established to protect Indian nations' power in adoption cases and keep Native children in Native homes, have come under fire by the conservative wing of the private adoption industry, which dislikes conforming to the law, arguing that it unconstitutionally discriminates based on race.[15] And the intractable problems associated with Indian poverty have persisted.

In 2011 the Occupy Wall Street movement galvanized and united people across racial divides after the 2009 economic crisis glaringly exposed the widening income divide between the "99 percent" at the bottom of the economic ladder and the 1 percent at the top. By occupying the centers of financial power, activists displayed their disdain for an exploitative capitalist system that creates inequality and perpetuates climate change through endless plunder of the natural world. Indigenous peoples were quick to point out, however, that from their perspective Wall Street (and other centers of financial power) was already occupied space. The problem, they emphasized, went beyond capitalism and in reality could be traced to the colonial roots of the United States. This proved to be an irreconcilable conflict in the Occupy movement.

Meanwhile, the battles in the global environmental movement raged on, as climate change became more and more connected to international Indigenous rights issues. Indigenous
peoples in North America began rising to the top as leaders in
the movement, especially as the Alberta tar-sands mining operation was exposed for its destructiveness to the environment
and the devastating effects it was having in First Nations communities. Then, under the conservative administration of then
prime minister Stephen Harper, in 2011, the Canadian government announced that it was pulling out of the Kyoto Protocol,
the only international treaty in existence to address climate
change. The following year, a series of anti-Indian, anti-
environment omnibus bills proposed by the Harper regime
gave birth to a new movement, Idle No More (INM). INM began when four First Nations women in Saskatchewan mobilized
a social media campaign to combat the new laws.[16] At the same
time, coincidentally, Theresa Spence, chief of the Attawapiskat
First Nation, launched a hunger strike to force a conversation
with Prime Minister Harper about what she characterized as a
state of emergency on her reserve.[17] The two separate incidents
quickly became conflated, even though Spence had nothing to
do with the INM actions of the Saskatchewan women. The grass-
roots INM became seen as an Indigenous rights movement, but
its message had broad appeal beyond the Indigenous world.[18]

INM went international when round dance flash mobs began
popping up in shopping malls and other public places all over
Canada and the United States, and people in other countries
used social media in strong support of INM and Chief Spence. In
the United States, Native Americans had in the meantime been
staging large demonstrations against the Keystone XL Pipeline,
a proposed pipeline to transport tar-sands oil from Canada to
the Gulf Coast. Particularly problematic was a route through the

Midwest in Lakota and other Indian territories, endangering the largest underground aquifer in the country. In a historic show of solidarity in 2014, Native people, ranchers, and other landowners formed the Cowboy Indian Alliance and gathered together in Washington, DC, for five days to implore President Obama to reject the pipeline plan. Reminiscent of the Alcatraz Island occupation a generation earlier, the multicultural, multiethnic coalition had celebrity support with the high-profile participation of rock star Neil Young and actress Daryl Hannah.

The same year, in New York City, the Peoples' Climate March drew tens of thousands of people (preceding the historic UN World Conference on Indigenous Peoples), led by the Indigenous Bloc, which included former congressman Dennis Kucinich and actors Leonardo DiCaprio and Mark Ruffalo.[19] And in a moment flashing back to the 1973 Academy Awards, in his acceptance speech in 2016 for a Golden Globe award, DiCaprio said that he "wanted to share this award with all First Nations people represented in this film and all Indigenous communities around the world. It is time we recognize your history and that we protect your Indigenous lands from corporate interests and people out there that would exploit them. It is time that we heard your voice and protected this planet for future generations."[20]

In other words, in the twenty-first century, Native American political struggles have merged with a global Indigenous rights movement that itself is inextricably bound to the global environmental and climate justice movements. These movements now involve people worldwide. American Indians have always been, as the famous legal scholar Felix Cohen contended, the "miner's canary," reflecting the rise and fall of society's "democratic faith."[21] Today it is clear that Indigenous peoples everywhere are—and always have been—the miner's canary on a global scale. In a hyper-industrialized, super-exploitive world, what happens to Indigenous peoples will eventually happen to everyone. Still, as long as humankind is organized in the current state-based system, Indigenous peoples' fights for self-determination and the protection of their environments will always be with state governments.

The gains made in federal Indian policy since the early twentieth century could be said to be steady but fragile. Sometimes they are ephemeral and tenuous, and other times they are solid and substantial. The current policy of self-determination—now almost half a century old—seems here to stay, but Native people know that when it comes to Indian affairs, nothing is ever assured because of the built-in systems of white supremacy and settler domination. Gains made though legislation or executive order can always be crippled by judicial decisions from an ill-informed or politically conservative Supreme Court.[22] Legislation can be reversed in a shifting political climate through an aggressive exercise of the plenary power doctrine. What is certain is that when progress does occur, it is almost always because of Native people's proactive organizing to demand change. And as our examples demonstrate, those mobilizations rely on alliances with non-Native people. Inevitably this is a process of awareness-raising and education by transcending conventional historical narratives to include those from Native perspectives. And because centuries of colonialism cannot be expected to be undone in one generation or even one century, this process of decolonization must be seen as an ongoing, multigenerational prospect.

Engaging the sensibilities of well-intentioned onlookers and other stakeholders both political and nonpolitical, narratives of Indian plight tend to invoke a sense of pity and emphasize victimhood. This risks robbing Native people of their own agency and can result in the underestimation of the ability of Native people to be self-determining. As is true in all relationships, the relationship between American Indians and non-Natives is a two-way street, where reciprocity implies mutual responsibility. Simply stated, the work of achieving justice for American Indian peoples involves everyone, Indigenous and settler alike, because colonization dehumanizes both the colonized and the colonizer. Wanda Caslin and Denise Breton write, "Colonization denies entire peoples of these inherent human rights and the empowering responsibilities that go with them. Colonialism feels bad and punishing because that's what it is. If, as is often said, we cannot get to a good place in a bad way, then we cannot get to a good society or a good relationship between peoples as long as colonialism is the dominant model."[23]

Historical Time Line[1]

Precolonial—According to conventional science, humans begin migrating from Asia to North America thirty thousand to forty thousand years ago. The Bering Strait land bridge theory postulates that humans crossed a hypothetical land bridge and arrived south of the Canadian ice sheets 16,000 years ago, while the "Clovis First" model confirms human habitation in North America (current New Mexico) 11,500 years ago. However, recent discoveries confirm the existence of humans in South America at least twenty thousand years ago, upending the Clovis model. By twelve thousand years ago—and very likely earlier—Indians lived in all the unglaciated areas of the entire hemisphere. Competing and ever-changing theories make the dates for human habitation in North America a moving target and ignore the fact that two of the seven agricultural civilizations in the world originated there, which created food plants—such as corn, tomato, squash, pumpkin, and cacao.

9000 BC—*Agriculture begins in North America.*

4500 BC—*Monumental building begins in the Mississippi Valley.*

750 BC—*Monumental temples are built in the Ohio Valley.*

Ca. 1000—*Leif Erikson and a crew of other Norse explorers are the first-known Europeans to sail to North America. They settle in a region of today's southeastern Canada, but the settlement ultimately* *fails and the Vikings disappear, leaving behind artifacts that are discovered at L'Anse-aux-Meadows in Newfoundland in 1963.*

AD 200–1400—*The Hohokam culture—predecessors of the Tohono O'odham people in the Gila and Salt River region of today's southern Arizona—is a technologically advanced agricultural civilization made possible by a complex system of irrigation canals. They also build large ball courts similar to those of the Mayans, for a game played with the first rubber balls known in the world.*

AD 600–1400—*Cahokia, one of the world's largest cities in its time (located in today's Illinois), with some fifty thousand people at its peak, is part of a larger group of Indigenous peoples known as the Mississippians, predecessors of today's so-called Five Civilized Tribes—Cherokee, Creek, Chickasaw, Choctaw, and Seminole— among others.*

1390—*The Haudenosaunee (league of the five nations of the Iroquois—Seneca, Oneida, Onondaga, Mohawk, and Cayuga) is founded in what is now northern New York State and southern Ontario. Later, in 1712, the Tuscaroras will join the league.*

1400—*Some of the Athabaskan-speaking peoples of the sub-Arctic region in the Northwest (Alaska and Canada) move to what is now the US Southwest and divide into two large groups, Navajos (Diné) and Apaches.*

1452—*Pope Nicholas V issues Dum Diversas, authorizing Portugal to reduce Muslims, pagans, and all non-Christians to perpetual slavery and to seize their property.*

1455—*The same pope issues Romanus Pontifex, granting a monopoly on the African slave trade to Portugal and reinforcing the Europeans' power to enslave non-Christian Native peoples wherever they are found and seize their lands. This is the onset of four centuries of transatlantic trade in enslaved Africans.*

1492—Columbus arrives in the Caribbean believing he has found the Spice Islands of Indonesia ("East Indies"), which he calls the West Indies. He completes four round-trips between 1492 and 1498, wreaking death and destruction among the three million Taino residents of Hispaniola (today's Dominican Republic), establishing a trade in Indian slaves that would last over a century, and launching a genocide that would result in the Indigenous depopulation of much of the Caribbean, repopulated with enslaved Africans.

1493—Pope Alexander VI issues the bull Inter Caetera, granting the newly "discovered" lands in America to Spain.

1503—Fishermen from England begin trading with the North Atlantic maritime peoples (Abenakis, Passamaquoddy, Micmacs, Penobscots, and others), exchanging metal tools and cloth for furs and food. Soon French fishermen are trading with peoples of the Great Lakes region.

1513—The Spanish governor of Puerto Rico, Ponce de Leon, is driven away from Florida by the Calusas. He will return as a conquistador in 1521 with an organized colonizing mission, which will fail when the Calusas once again drive the Spanish out, mortally wounding the conquistador.

1519—The conquistador Hernando Cortés and four hundred armored and mounted men land at Yucatán when Mexico is in the midst of civil war. From the huge and majestic city of Tenochtitlán, the Aztec state rules over some thirty million people in greater Mexico, enforcing onerous tribute payments on the Indigenous farmers. Cortés allies with those attempting to overthrow the regime, and within two years the ancient and great civilization is reduced to ruins in one of the most horrific genocidal campaigns in history.

1525–39—A small Spanish exploring party, led by Cabeza de Vaca, seeking "seven cities of gold," barely survives the journey from Florida to Texas, with only de Vaca and an enslaved African, Estevanico, continuing to Mexico City. They claim to have sighted the cities de Vaca sought. This will lead to the mounting of the Coronado expedition into New Mexico three years later, where Estevanico is killed when he is sent ahead to scout and enters Zuni Pueblo without permission. The friar with the expedition returns to Mexico falsely claiming that the Pueblo civilization of the Rio Grande is wealthier than the Aztecs or the Incas, which makes future invasion only a matter of time.

1565—The Spanish set up the first European permanent settlement in what is now the United States. St. Augustine, Florida, functions as a base camp for further incursions on the continent.

1587—English colonists unsuccessfully attempt to create a settlement on Roanoke Island (off what is now mainland North Carolina).

1598—Don Juan Oñate, leading five hundred soldiers and families from Mexico, invades Pueblo lands in present-day New Mexico. The people of the city-state of Acoma, located on a steep rock mesa, resist, and the Spanish siege of Acoma ends with 800 Acomas slaughtered, while 570 are captured and put on trial, the men sentenced to having their right hands cut off and the women indentured into servitude. The Spanish colonizers impose a colonial system of domination and exploitation, brutalizing the Pueblo peoples throughout Spain's rule in the Southwest, drastically reducing the population and number of autonomous Pueblo towns.

1607—The first permanent English settlement in what is now the United States is established at Jamestown, Virginia, on the lands of the Powhatan confederacy of Indigenous nations. Within two years, there is full-scale war, which continues off and on, while the London stock company financing the colony begins a lucrative trade in Indian tobacco, enticing a flood of English settlers, who instead of purchasing land from the Powhatans and clearing the forests and planting crops, attack and drive them out of their fields, burning their towns. Warfare continues until 1644, with the destruction of the Powhatan confederacy, leaving thousands of homeless and starving refugees. This marks the pattern of British settler-colonialism as they seize the Eastern Seaboard over a period of nearly two centuries.

1616–19—Following an exploratory mapping of southern New England by John Smith, a deadly epidemic wipes out a majority of Native peoples where the *Mayflower* will arrive.

1620—The *Mayflower*, financed by a British corporation, lands at the site of the Wampanoag (Pokanoket) village known as Patuxet, which the pilgrims rename New Plymouth.

1621—The pilgrims meet the sachem leader Massasoit and the English-speaking Squanto, who teaches them how to farm the Indian way, saving them from certain starvation. Massasoit negotiates a treaty of mutual protection with the colonists.

1621–60—More than forty thousand English Puritan (Calvinist) settlers flood Native lands in New England, initially drawn by stories of the local Indians being friendly with the Pilgrims. The Massachusetts Bay Colony is chartered, and settlers assume, when they acquire land from Indian communities for payment, that it is then their private property, but Indigenous nations in the Americas do not recognize individual private property and consider the money to be payment for use rights. The original inhabitants expect to continue to use the land for fishing and taking game.

1636–37—The Pequots' attempt to drive the English squatters out of their territory, the Connecticut Valley, with organized

English militias burning villages. Captain John Mason launches a militia attack that kills over seven hundred Pequots—men, women, and children.

1638—The English Puritans, in dominating Connecticut, force the Quinnipiacs onto a much reduced land base, the first Indian reservation. The Indians are ruled by an English agent and prohibited from leaving the reservation or allowing other Indians inside. They are not allowed to bear arms and are forced to convert to Christianity, acknowledging that their own beliefs are Satanic.

1675–76—The first major war between the English settlers in New England and the Native people breaks out, known as King Philip's War. A coalition of Native communities including Wampanoags, Narragansetts, Nipmucks, Mohegans, and Podunks attacks more than half the ninety English towns in Massachusetts and Rhode Island, wiping out twelve of them. Puritan militias form, with their ministers urging them to "exterminate the savage Canaanites." A bloodbath begins, a war of extermination. The bloodied and mutilated bodies of Native people are dubbed "redskins" by the Puritans. Those not killed are sold into slavery in the West Indies.

1675–76—Bacon's Rebellion is an uprising led by a member of the Virginia elite but composed of former indentured servants, both black and white. Although their rebellion would be heralded by multiculturalists in the twentieth century as a moment of racial unity, their goal was to pressure the Virginia colonial authorities to forcibly remove Indigenous farmers and distribute the land to the rebels. The rebellion is finally put down, but it leads authorities in 1691 to banish whites who intermarry with Indians, blacks, or anyone of mixed race.

1680—The Pueblo Revolt, inspired by religious leader Popé and joined by Navajos, Apaches, and Genízaros (the name for mestizos in New Mexico), drives the Spanish settlers, officials, priests, and soldiers out of Santa Fe. Peace and freedom ensues in the region for twelve years, at which time the Spanish return in full force and rule for another century.

1700—The encroachment of Spanish, French, and British colonists in North America leads many sedentary Native peoples to acquire horses and migrate to the Great Plains for buffalo hunting, particularly the Comanches and the Sioux.

1701—After six decades of warfare in northern New York, French Canada, and the Great Lakes region, exacerbated by French and British competition for domination in the region, with dozens of Native nations allied with one side or the other, a certain peace is reached, with greater domination of trade by the European powers and aggressive conversion by Christian missionaries.

1712—The Tuscaroras of the area that becomes North Carolina fight against English slave traders and choose to migrate to New York, where they became the sixth nation of the Iroquois Confederacy.

1737—The Lenape (Delaware) people who are indigenous to what is now New Jersey, Delaware, Maryland, Pennsylvania, and southern New York, are forcibly removed from Pennsylvania.

1754–60—The French and Indian War between Britain and France (the North American theater of the European Seven Years' War) leads to France's loss of most of its claimed territory in North America.

1763—The British Royal Proclamation of 1763 limits English expansion of settlements over the eastern mountain chain into the Indigenous farmlands of the Ohio Valley, becoming a major contributing factor to the decision of settlers to fight for independence from Britain in order to form their own empire.

In 1765, to raise funds for the cost of policing the proclamation line, the British Parliament enacts the Stamp Act, which riles the settlers.

1763–66—Pontiac, leader of the Ottawa Nation in the Great Lakes region, puts together a large alliance of Native nations and communities to prevent the entrance of British agents who intend to seize all the French forts and outposts in the area. The alliance succeeds in holding back the British until they run out of weapons and ammunition, when all the communities are forced into peace treaties with the British.

1766—Land speculators and companies begin to map Indian lands in the Ohio Valley. Among the investors are future US presidents George Washington and Thomas Jefferson.

1769—Daniel Boone opens a route from Virginia into Kentucky, part of the Ohio Country, in defiance of the 1763 proclamation. Settler squatters flood the farmlands of the Shawnees and Cherokees.

1769—Spanish Franciscan priests under the leadership of Junipero Serra use the Spanish army to attack, capture, and bring in the Native peoples, forcing them into labor in the prison-like missions in what is now California.

1774—The First Continental Congress is formed, one of its first acts being the appointment of a Committee on Indian Affairs to assure either Indigenous alliance or neutrality in the settlers' war of independence from Britain, but this wins over only the Delawares and the Oneidas under threats of total destruction. During the same year, the governor of the Virginia colony, Lord Dunmore, organizes a settler militia of three thousand to attack Shawnees in support of the illegal squatters in the Ohio Valley. The Shawnees form a confederation to defend the territory from invasion, which persists until it is crushed in 1812.

1776—The Declaration of Independence states among its reasons for secession: "He [the king] has excited domestic insurrections amongst us, and has endeavoured to bring on the inhabitants of our frontiers, the merciless Indian Savages, whose known rule of warfare, is an undistinguished destruction of all ages, sexes and conditions."

1778—The United States signs its first treaty with a Native nation, the Delaware Nation, to gain access to Delaware trade and create a military and political alliance during the Revolutionary War.

1783—The Treaty of Paris is signed, with Britain granting independence to the United States, with no mention of Indian rights. The bargaining power available to Native nations is down to a trickle, as that of their French and British allies has diminished or disappeared.

1787—The Constitutional Convention enacts the Northwest Ordinance, a plan to take the Indigenous peoples' land and farms in the Ohio Valley for Euro-American settlement and statehood, with empty promises for those to be displaced: "The utmost good faith shall always be observed towards the Indians; their lands and property shall never be taken from them without their consent; and, in their property, rights, and liberty, they shall never be invaded or disturbed, unless in just and lawful wars authorized by Congress; but laws founded in justice and humanity, shall from time to time be made for preventing wrongs being done to them, and for preserving peace and friendship with them." The Bill of Rights amended to the Constitution famously includes the Second Amendment that empowers settler-militias and guarantees the right of every settler to be armed.

1789—Federal Indian affairs are placed under the auspices of the War Department (which will become the Department of

Defense after World War II). The Office of Indian Affairs will be formed in 1824, remaining in the War Department.

1790–99—Settlers in the Ohio Valley are stunned by the gigantic earth works and Native antiquities and artifacts, which they loot. Washington and Jefferson pack their mansions with these stolen items.

1791—The Shawnee Confederation (fourteen allied Native nations) under the leadership of Blue Jacket and Little Turtle defeat a force of fourteen hundred militiamen organized by the US governor of the Northwest Territory. Tecumseh fights in this battle and soon rises to leadership of the confederation.

1793—Congress appropriates funds for the founding of the US Army to support militias in their attempts to dislodge the resident Indians in the Ohio Valley. The following year, twenty-two hundred army infantrymen along with a full cavalry and fifteen hundred Kentucky militiamen will attack the Shawnee Confederation, and the Battle of Fallen Timbers ensues, making clear that the confederation is unable to prevail in an all-out war. In 1795 the allied Native nations will sign the Greenville Treaty of Peace, giving up some land in exchange for a US-enforced boundary between Indigenous territory and US territory. The treaty will also stipulate that only nations can cede land, not individual Indians. However, the Northwest Territory governor, William Henry Harrison, ignores the treaty and continues military pressure against the Indians.

1794—Jay's Treaty between British Canada and the United States establishes the border between Canada and the United States. It allows the British to maintain their forts in the Northwest Territory and guarantees the right of the Indigenous inhabitants to move freely within their territories that now overlap the Euro-American border, without paying duties. This treaty remains in effect today.

1797—The nations of the Iroquois Confederacy retain only fragments of their once expansive territories.

1803—The United States purchases from Napoleon the "Louisiana territory," which contains not only what is now Louisiana and the Mississippi Valley, but the vast middle of the continent, eight hundred thousand square miles, doubling the territorial claim of the new North American republic, opening up a new wave of western expansion into Indian lands.

1801–15—The Barbary Wars transpire, the first US wars overseas. "From the Halls of Montezuma to the shores of Tripoli," the first line of the official hymn of the US Marine Corps (composed and adopted soon after the US 1846 invasion of Mexico) will refer back to the First Barbary War, when President Jefferson dispatched the navy to invade North Africa. The ostensible goal was to force Tripoli to release US sailors it held hostage and to end "pirate" attacks on US merchant ships. In 1816, the wars in the Mediterranean will end with US victory when Pasha Yusuf Karamanli, ruler of Tripoli, agrees not to exact fees from US ships entering its territorial waters. The United States is an overseas imperialist power from its inception.

1805–6—The Lewis and Clark military expedition takes place. Soon after acquiring Louisiana, President Jefferson commissions a group of army volunteers under the command of Captain Meriwether Lewis and Second Lieutenant William Clark. Their task is to map the newly acquired territory and collect information on the Native nations present in every part of the territory. They impress multilingual Sacajawea, Shoshone wife of a French fur trader, into service as interpreter and guide on the 7,689-mile trek.

1806–13—Tecumseh rightly surmises that the United States intends to take all the land of the Northwest Territory and drive out the Indigenous inhabitants. With his brother, the religious leader Tenskwatawa (the Prophet), he envisions a new alliance from the Great Lakes to the Gulf of Mexico. They establish a new village, Prophetstown, as the capital of the alliance, attracting Shawnees, Wyandots, Delawares, Ottawas, and others. Tecumseh travels all the way to Florida, organizing along the way with the Creeks and Seminoles. They build channels of communication and trade throughout the interior. The alliance includes escaped slaves and free Blacks, along with errant citizens of Spain and France, as well as people from all of the southern Native nations. In 1811, while Tecumseh is in Florida, William Henry Harrison invades Prophetstown with nine hundred troops, burning all the buildings and granaries and forcing a treaty of cession. But Tecumseh continues organizing into Canada, allying for a time with British forces in the War of 1812. Tecumseh is killed in battle in 1813, and British support evaporates at the end of the war. The Creek and southern alliance, the Creek Confederacy, continues operating in the South, ending up in a new fortified center in the Everglades of Spanish-held Florida.

1814—Creeks are decimated at the Battle of Horseshoe Bend in Alabama by a Tennessee militia founded and headed by Andrew Jackson, a wealthy slave owner. Surviving Red Stick Creek warriors join the Seminole resistance in the Everglades.

1817–18—The First Seminole War begins after federal authorities enter Spanish Florida illegally in an attempt to recover plantation owners' "property": former African slaves. Under the leadership of Osceola, the Seminoles repel the invasion. In 1818 President James Monroe orders Andrew Jackson, by then a major general in the US Army, to lead three thousand soldiers into Florida to crush the Seminoles and retrieve the Africans among them. The expedition destroys a number of Seminole settlements and captures the Spanish fort at Pensacola, bringing down the Spanish government but failing to destroy Seminole guerrilla resistance. The Seminoles refuse to hand over any former slaves. The United States will wage three wars against the Seminole Nation in the Everglades between 1817 and 1858. The prolonged and fierce Second Seminole War (1835–42), while Jackson is president, will be the longest war waged by the United States up to the Vietnam War. The Seminoles will never surrender, and they still hold their territory in Florida.

1823—*Johnson v. M'Intosh* is the first Supreme Court case of the Marshall Trilogy, the foundation of all subsequent federal Indian law. It first articulates the doctrine of discovery.

1830—President Jackson signs the Indian Removal Act, authorizing the president to carve up Indigenous peoples' territories west of the Mississippi in order to resettle the southeastern Native peoples on it and creating "Indian Territory," later Oklahoma, which allows for the rapid development of the Cotton Kingdom in the Southeast.

1831—In *Cherokee v. Georgia*, the second case in the Supreme Court's Marshall Trilogy, the court affirms the sovereignty of the Cherokee Nation to the ire of President Jackson, who refuses to follow the decision and initiates the removal of the "Five Civilized Tribes" (Cherokees, Choctaws, Creeks, Chickasaws, and Seminoles), so named for their adoption of US-style government.

1832—*Worcester v. Georgia*, the third case in the Marshall Trilogy, holds that Indians are domestic dependent nations, not foreign nations.

1838—The Trail of Tears begins. Cherokee, Creek, Chickasaw, Choctaw, and Seminole peoples are forced to walk over one thousand miles from their homelands in the Southeast to

Indian Territory (today's Oklahoma), resulting in the deaths of over ten thousand.

1848—The United States signs the Treaty of Guadalupe Hidalgo after the cessation of a two-year war against Mexico, which loses half its territory to the United States, beginning a new reign of terror against California Indians as the gold rush takes off the following year. The treaty mandates cooperation between the two countries to destroy the now cross-border Apache and Navajo Nations.

1862—The Dakota Sioux resistance to settlers taking their land ends with the mass hanging of thirty-eight Dakota men, the largest execution in US history.

1864—The Navajos are forcibly removed from their homelands in Arizona and forcibly marched by irregular troops led by Kit Carson to southeastern New Mexico, where half of them die while incarcerated, a traumatic event Navajos call the Long Walk.

1871—Congress unilaterally ends treaty-making with Indians.

1879—The Carlisle Indian Industrial School is established in Pennsylvania, the prototype for the many militaristic federal boarding schools that will be set up across the continent soon after, augmented by dozens of Christian missionary boarding schools. Sent to faraway boarding schools, children are subject to an educational regime designed to teach them Euro-American ways (under the philosophy "kill the Indian, save the man") and train them for low-level service jobs, damaging generations of Native children into the mid-twentieth century before the schools were reformed or closed.

1882—Helen Hunt Jackson publishes *A Century of Dishonor*, signaling emerging pro-Indian sentiment in the country, which leads, however, to a policy of assimilation and privatization of the Native estates.

1887—The Dawes Act is passed in Congress, sanctioning a policy of assimilation through privatization of Indian reservation lands. Lands are carved up into 80-acre and 160-acre allotments designated for individual farming and ranching. "Surplus" lands are opened for white settlement.

1890—Decades of armed Sioux resistance, led by Crazy Horse and Sitting Bull, among others, end in the massacre at Wounded Knee, leaving hundreds of unarmed and Sioux refugees dead. It is classified by the US military as a victory for the Seventh Cavalry, with dozens of Congressional Medals of Honor bestowed on the soldiers. Native resistance is generally seen as over.

1911—The Society of American Indians (SAI), America's first pan-Indian organization, forms to lobby for civil rights and assimilation for Indians.

1923—Deskaheh, leader and spokesperson for the Iroquois Confederation of Canada, goes to Geneva, Switzerland, to present the confederation's long-standing dispute with the Canadian government to the League of Nations.

1924—Congress passes the Indian Citizenship Act realizing the lobbying efforts of the SAI.

1928—The Meriam Report condemns the federal assimilation policy for causing intractable poverty on Indian reservations.

1934—The Wheeler-Howard Act (Indian Reorganization Act) signals a new Indian policy direction, allowing for newly organized tribal governments under strict federal supervision.

1944—The National Congress of American Indians emerges from the remnants of the SAI.

1946—The Indian Claims Commission is formed to monetarily settle Indian land claims, not to return lands.

1953—Congress passes House Concurrent Resolution 108, the Termination Act, in order to officially terminate the federal government's treaty relationship to Indian nations, the reservations to be dissolved, attempting to once and for all absorb Indians into mass society. Over one hundred tribes are terminated over the next few years. The federal relocation program encourages subsidized movement of Indians on reservations to designated urban areas, within a decade creating a large urban Indian population. Only after two decades of Native organizing is termination stopped.

1957—The International Labour Organization adopts conventions concerning the protection of Indigenous peoples, but they are inherently paternalistic and assimilationist.

1960—The National Indian Youth Council is founded in Albuquerque.

1964—Pacific Northwest tribes begin staging fish-ins in a move to get the United States to enforce their treaty-based rights to salmon fishing. This will culminate in the 1975 Boldt decision (*United States v. Washington*) finding in favor of the Native people to fish in their traditional waters even if not on reservation land.

1968—The American Indian Civil Rights Act is passed to give a measure of individual civil liberties to Indians. The American Indian Movement is founded in Minneapolis, modeled on black civil rights groups and made up largely from the urban Indian population.

1969—The two-and-a-half-year occupation of Alcatraz Island (San Francisco) begins, drawing national and international attention to Indian rights concerns.

1970—President Nixon condems the termination policy, announcing a new federal policy of Indian self-determination, and signs into law the return of the sacred lands of Blue Lake to Taos Pueblo.

1971—The Alaska Native Claims Settlement Act is passed, which turns Alaska Native nations into corporations and extinguishes 90 percent of their claims to land in exchange for forty million acres of land and almost $1 billion.

1972—President Nixon signs into law the Indian Self-Determination and Education Act, reversing the previously assimilationist termination policy and giving tribal governments greater control over their affairs. In response, hundreds of Indian protesters caravan to Washington, DC, in the "Trail of Broken Treaties" to present their Twenty Point Position Paper to Nixon and occupy the Bureau of Indian Affairs building for almost a week.

1973—The American Indian Movement leads a seventy-one-day occupation of Wounded Knee in South Dakota. Marlon Brando sends Sacheen Littlefeather to reject an Oscar at the Academy Awards, drawing attention to Hollywood's treatment of Indians and showing solidarity with the Wounded Knee protesters.

1974—The American Indian Movement Organizes a conference of thousands to form the International Indian Treaty Council.

1975—Congress passes the Indian Self-Determination and Education Assistance Act, giving tribal governments greater control over their affairs.

1977—Leonard Peltier is convicted of murdering an FBI agent on the Pine Ridge Indian Reservation and sentenced to two consecutive terms of life in prison, despite evidence that supports his innocence, making him widely viewed as a political prisoner.

1977—At United Nations headquarters in Geneva, Switzerland, the NGO Conference discrimination of Indigenous Populations in America is held, producing the "Draft Declaration of the Principles for the Defence of the Indigenous Nations and Peoples of the Western Hemisphere."

1978—Congress passes the American Indian Freedom of Religion Act and the Indian Child Welfare Act.

1978—In *Santa Clara Pueblo v. Martinez*, the Supreme Court affirms the right of tribal governments to determine their own membership, a strong show of support for tribal sovereignty.

1982—The Working Group on Indigenous Populations is established in the United Nations, the beginning of the UN Draft Declaration on the Rights of Indigenous Peoples.

1988—The Indian Gaming Regulatory Act is passed to support tribal economic development.

1989—The International Labour Organization adopts Convention 169, the only international treaty to consider the problems of Indigenous peoples.

1990—The Native American Graves and Repatriation Act is passed to facilitate processes of repatriating Native American remains and burial artifacts, further bolstering tribal sovereignty.

1994—Congress passes the Tribal Self-Governance Act, creating a new compacting process between tribal governments and the BIA for greater tribal control of financial resources.

1996—Eloise Cobell (Blackfeet) files a lawsuit against the US Department of the Interior and US Department of the Treasury for over a century of mismanagement of Indian trust accounts.

1996—The remains of an ancient male skeleton, which will become known as Kennewick Man and the Ancient One, is found on the banks of the Columbia River. It's speculated that the Ancient One was Caucasian, igniting a two-decade controversy over the how the remains are to be handled and who they belong to.

2000—The Bureau of Indian Affairs, via Assistant Secretary for Indian Affairs Kevin Gover (Pawnee), delivers an official apology for its wrongs against American Indians.

2007—After over two decades of deliberations, the UN General Assembly passes the Declaration on the Rights of Indigenous Peoples, with four no votes coming from Australia, New Zealand, Canada, and the United States, which all later will change to yes.

2009—Congress passes a resolution of apology to American Indians. Buried in a defense appropriations bill, the resolution receives little notice.

2010—President Obama signs the Claims Resolution Act settling the fourteen-year-long Cobell lawsuit. It is considered the largest settlement by the US government in history.

2010—Under Obama, the United States becomes the last member state to endorse the Declaration on the Rights of Indigenous Peoples.

2012—The international Indigenous activist movement Idle No More is born after a series of anti-Indian and anti-environment legislation is passed under the Harper administration in Canada.

2014—The US Senate confirms the first Native American woman, Diane Humetewa (Hopi), to a federal judgeship.

2014—In June thousands of Indigenous and Fourth World nations' representatives from all over the world gather in Alta, Norway, to collectively prepare a statement for the upcoming UN World Conference on Indigenous Peoples (WCIP), the most significant gathering of Indigenous peoples in history.

The statement is a list of recommendations for UN member states' own WCIP Outcome Document on how they can improve their relations with Indigenous peoples. In September, the World Conference on Indigenous Peoples is the first high-level plenary meeting for Indigenous issues in the UN, but the WCIP Outcome Document ultimately ignores many of the Alta statement's recommendations. The WCIP is seen by many as an important step forward, while others are highly critical of its limitations.

2015—DNA analysis determines that Kennewick Man is genetically more related to the Colville Indians than to any other known group in the world.

2015—In a speech in Santa Cruz, Bolivia, Pope Francis delivers an apology for the Catholic Church's sins against all Indigenous peoples. Two months later he canonizes Father Junipero Serra despite widespread opposition in Indian country.

Acknowledgments

No one writes a book without a team of people behind them, influencing them along the way. Some are on the front lines involved with the actual book itself and some provide the intellectual or personal foundation. Foremost on the front line was our awesome, inimitable editor Gayatri Patnaik, without whose discerning editorial eye and wide open mind this book would've suffered, and we thank her and the rest of the staff at Beacon Press for making this book happen.

Thanks to the faculty in the Native American studies program at the University of New Mexico (UNM) who continually mentor and pave a path of Native scholarship, especially Gregory Cajete, Lloyd Lee, Tiffany Lee, Beverly Singer, Mary Bowannie, Thomas Birdbear, Derrick Lente, and Maria Williams. Thanks also to the American studies faculty at UNM (past and present), who work hard to give Native people a voice in the field: Alex Lubin, Alyosha Goldstein, David Correia, Jennifer Nez Denetdale, Michael Trujillo, Gerald Vizenor, and amazing Native doctoral students and friends Nick Estes and Melanie Yazzie. At UNM, thanks also to Anne Calhoun and Chris Sims in the Department of Language, Literacy, and Sociocultural Studies. *Pilamiya* to Terri Flowerday in the College of Education for daring to indigenize educational psychology and for being an irreplaceable friend.

Thank you to Rudy Rÿser at the Center for World Indigenous Studies (CWIS) for his fearlessness and tireless dedication to Indigenous geopolitics, and to his wife, Leslie Korn, for her amazing work to raise the cultural awareness of providers of mental health care everywhere. Thanks also to Heidi Bruce at CWIS for being a fantastic writing partner and coworker. At Indian Country Today Media Network, Indian country's premier voice to the world, thank you to Ray Halbritter, Bob Roe, Ray Cook, Theresa Braine, Chris Napolitano, Vincent Schilling, Gayle Courey Toensing, and Ken Poulisse for your support and for giving Indian people a platform. We appreciate our colleagues in and beyond the Native American and Indigenous Studies Association for the brilliant scholarship which influences so much of this book: Jeani O'Brien, Philip Deloria, Kim Tallbear, Ranjit Arab at University of Washington Press, Colville sister Laurie Arnold, Coll Thrush, Joanne Barker, Brendan Lindsay, Eric Cheyfitz, James Brooks, Patrick Wolfe, Vine Deloria Jr., Robert Williams Jr., and all those present, both physically and spiritually, too numerous to mention.

Finally, a book cannot be written without family and friends who provide love and support in all kinds of ways. Dina thanks Katie Alvord for over twenty years of friendship and inspiration as a writer, Geri DeStefano-Webre and Sissy Gilio for their unfaltering sisterhood, and most of all Tom Whitaker for being the best of the best.

Roxanne thanks most of all her daughter and best friend, Michelle Callarman, and her many nieces and nephews (and grand- and great-grandnieces and nephews) in Oklahoma, Washington, Louisiana, California, Nevada, New Mexico, New York, Florida, and Cambodia, and she is grateful for the support and counsel of friends Chude Allen, Anne Weills, Rachel Jackson, Andrew Curley, Nanabaa Beck, John Mage, Simon Ortiz, and Starry Krueger. She remembers the late Lee Roy Chapman and Martin Legassick, thanks her colleagues of the Indigenous World Association—Kenneth Deer, Petuuche Gilbert, Mililani Trask, June Lorenzo, and Judith LeBlanc, and is grateful for many others.

NOTES

INTRODUCTION

1. Michel Foucault, *Society Must Be Defended: Lectures at the Collège de France, 1975–76* (New York: Picador, 1997), 47–48.
2. For more on structural violence, see more generally the work of Paul Farmer such as "An Anthropology of Structural Violence," *Current Anthropology* 45, no. 3 (June 2004), and Tracy Kidder's Pulitzer Prize–winning *Mountains Beyond Mountains: The Quest of Dr. Paul Farmer, a Man Who Would Cure the World* (New York: Random House, 2009).
3. For more on spiritual appropriation, see Lisa Aldred's "Plastic Shamans and Astroturf Sun Dances: New Age Commercialization of Native American Spirituality," *American Indian Quarterly* 24, no. 3 (Summer 2000): 329–52, or the extensive work on white shamanism by Wendy Rose.
4. "Indian" is in quotes because it is now widely known that Iron Eyes Cody was not Indian but a first-generation Sicilian American.
5. See Michael Yellow Bird and Waziyatawin Angela Wilson's *For Indigenous Eyes Only: A Decolonization Handbook* (Santa Fe: School of American Research, 2005) for their work on the miseducation of Indian children.
6. Timothy Lintner, "The Savage and the Slave: Critical Race Theory, Racial Stereotyping, and the Teaching of American History," *Journal of Social Studies Research* 28, no. 1 (2004): 27–32.
7. Sarah Shear et al., "Manifesting Destiny: Re/presentations of Indigenous Peoples in K–12 U.S. History Standards," *Theory and Research in Social Education* 43 (2015): 68–101.
8. Allan Johnson coined the term "systems of privilege" in his book *Privilege, Power, and Difference* (Boston: McGraw-Hill, 2001).
9. See Michael Omi and Howard Winant's classic treatise on race, *Racial Formation in the United States*, 3rd ed. (New York: Routledge, 2015).
10. For more on critical whiteness studies, see Robin DiAngelo, especially "White Fragility: Why It's So Hard to Talk to White People About Racism," Good Men Project, April 9, 2015, http://goodmenproject.com/featured -content/white-fragility-why-its-so-hard-to-talk-to-white-people -about-racism-twlm/#sthash.ns7dgYfo.dpuf.

MYTH 1: "ALL THE REAL INDIANS DIED OFF"

1. Occasionally throughout this book we make distinctions based on a frame-work known as Fourth World theory. Simply stated, Fourth World theory makes distinctions between states (as in nation-states) and Indigenous peoples as nations. From a Fourth World perspective, nations are far older than the modern state, which didn't come into existence until 1648 with the Treaty of Westphalia. Thus the term "nation-state" can be more ac-curately replaced with simply "state," whereas Indigenous peoples, due to their longevity, are more than just "tribes," "nomads," "peasants," "primi-tive people," and so forth. They are nations. These designations—"state" and "nation"—recognize cultural differences and the existence (or not) of people as political entities.

2. Countries in this category would include not just all in the Western Hemi-sphere but also Australia and New Zealand, all of which have significant Indigenous populations. Benedict Anderson, *Imagined Communities: Reflections on the Origin and Spread of Nationalism* (New York: Verso, 2006).

3. They also exploited human resources, resulting in the transatlantic slave trade, which for the most part benefited their exploits in the Americas.

4. Patrick Wolfe, "Settler Colonialism and the Elimination of the Native," *Journal of Genocide Research* 8, no. 4 (December 2006): 387–409.

5. Ibid., 388.

6. Jeani O'Brien, *Firsting and Lasting: Writing Indians Out of Existence in New England* (Minneapolis: University of Minnesota Press, 2010), xxii.

MYTH 2: "INDIANS WERE THE FIRST IMMIGRANTS TO THE WESTERN HEMISPHERE"

1. Simon Moya-Smith, "Harvard Professor Confirms Bering Strait Theory Is Not Fact," Indian Country Today Media Network, July 31, 2012, http://indiancountrytodaymedianetwork.com/2012/07/31/harvard-professor-confirms-bering-strait-theory-not-fact.

2. Heather Pringle, "The First Americans: Mounting Evidence Prompts Researchers to Reconsider the Peopling of the New World," *Scientific American*, October 2011, 36–45.

3. Jody Hey, "On the Number of New World Founders: A Population Genetic Portrait of the Peopling of the Americas," *PLOS Biology* 3, no. 6: e193, doi:10.1371/journal.pbio.003019.

4. Andrew Kitchen, Michael M. Miyamoto, and Connie J. Mulligan, "A Three-Stage Colonization Model for the Peopling of the Americas," *PLOS ONE* 3, no 2: doi: 10.1371/journal.pone.0001596. The study was updated shortly after its original publication, with a new analysis changing the number of the founding population to between one thousand and two thousand

people (instead of five thousand). See C. J. Mulligan, A. Kitchen, and M. M. Miyamoto, "Updated Three-Stage Model for the Peopling of the Americas," *PLoS ONE* 3, no. 9 (2008): e3199, doi:10.1371/ journal.pone.0003199.

5. Ker Than, "On Way to New World, First Americans Made a 10,000-Year Pit Stop," *National Geographic*, February 27, 2014, http://news.national geographic.com/news/2014/04/140227-native-americans-beringia -bering-strait-pit-stop.

6. Vine Deloria, *Red Earth, White Lies: Native Americans and the Myth of Scientific Fact* (Golden, CO: Fulcrum, 1997), 72.

7. Ibid., 24–25.

8. Annalee Newitz, "15,000-Year-Old Campsite in Texas Challenges Conventional Story of American Settlement," *io9*, March 24, 2011, http://io9.com /5785151/15000-year-old-campsite-in-texas-challenges-conventional -story-of-american-settlement.

9. Simon Romero, "Discoveries Challenge Beliefs on Humans' Arrival in the Americas," *New York Times*, March 27, 2014.

10. Alex Ewen, "Bering Strait Theory," parts 1–6, Indian Country Today Media Network, June 13, June 20, June 27, July 4, July 11, and July 19, 2014, http:// indiancountrytodaymedianetwork.com/.

11. Morten Rasmussen et al., "The Ancestry and Affiliations of Kennewick Man," *Nature*, June 18, 2015, http://www.nature.com/nature/journal/vnfv /ncurrent/full/nature14625.html.

12. The Native American Graves Protection and Repatriation Act (NAGPRA) was a significant human rights bill passed in 1990 in an effort to protect against the desecration of Native American graves, which have for centuries been subject to all manner of abuse not only by trophy hunters, but also by those who in the name of science dug up graves for study. NAGPRA mandates that the federal government protect Native American remains found on federal lands.

13. Douglas Preston, "The Kennewick Man Finally Freed to Share His Secrets," *Smithsonian*, September 2014, http://www.smithsonianmag.com/history /kennewick-man-finally-freed-share-his-secrets-180952462/?no-ist =&preview=_page%3D3_page%3D3&page=2.

14. Douglas W. Owsley and Richard L. Jantz, eds., *Kennewick Man: The Scientific Investigation of an Ancient American Skeleton* (College Station: Texas A&M University Press, 2014).

15. Bruce E. Johansen, *The Native Peoples of North America: A History*, vol. 1 (Westport, CT: Praeger, 2005).

16. "Other Migration Theories," Bering Land Bridge, National Park Service, http:// www.nps.gov/bela/learn/historyculture/other-migration-theories.htm.

MYTH 3: "COLUMBUS DISCOVERED AMERICA"

1. It is generally accepted that the Norwegian Leif Eriksson sailed to North America by way of Greenland hundreds of years before Columbus. It is thought that he settled temporarily in what is today Newfoundland, based on archaeological evidence uncovered in the 1960s. Other evidence of pre-Columbian journeys to North and South America includes massive Negroid and Caucasoid stone statues constructed by the Olmec civilization, strongly suggesting contact with Afro-Phoenician peoples between 1000 BC and AD 300; a map found in Turkey in 1513 showing coastline details of South America and Antarctica; and ancient Roman coins found by archaeologists all over the Americas, indicating voyages by Roman seafarers.

2. In one account in *Smithsonian* by Yale professor emeritus Edmund S. Morgan, for example, Columbus's enslavement, gruesome mass murders, and infanticide of Natives is recounted but seemingly excused this way: "Before we become too outraged at the behavior of Columbus and his followers, before we identify ourselves too easily with the lovable Arawaks, we have to ask whether we could really get along without greed and everything that goes with it. Yes, a few of us, a few eccentrics, might manage to live for a time like the Arawaks. But the modern world could not have put up with the Arawaks any more than the Spanish could. The story moves us, offends us, but perhaps the more so because we have to recognize ourselves not in the Arawaks but in Columbus and his followers." See Morgan, "Columbus' Confusion About the New World," *Smithsonian*, October 2009, http://www .smithsonianmag.com/people-places/columbus-confusion-about-the -new-world-140132422/#lPfaTK3wxY1RcXcv.99. The term "Age of Exploration" itself centers European history in a way that obscures many other cultures who, centuries before, had scientific and navigational knowledge far more advanced than the Europeans did when Columbus made his notorious first journey.

3. George E. Tinker and Mark Freeland, "Thief, Slave Trader, Murderer: Christopher Columbus and Caribbean Population Decline," *Wicazo Sa Review* 23, no. 1 (Spring 2008): 25–50.

4. Quoted in Howard Zinn, *A People's History of the United States* (New York: Harper Perennial Modern Classics, 2010), 1.

5. Ibid., 2.

6. Ibid., 4.

7. Ibid., 5.

8. All estimates come from Russell Thornton, "Population History of Native North Americans," in *A Population History of North America*, ed. Michael R. Haines and Richard H. Steckel (Cambridge, UK: Cambridge University Press, 2000), 12–46.

9. Ibid., 22, 44.

10. Ibid., 22.

11. David H. Getches, Charles F. Wilkinson, and Robert A. Williams Jr., *Cases and Materials on Federal Indian Law*, 5th ed. (St. Paul, MN: Thomson/ West, 2005).

12. Ibid., 42–43.

13. Steven T. Newcomb, *Pagans in the Promised Land: Decoding the Doctrine of Christian Discovery* (Golden, CO: Fulcrum, 2008), 84.

14. The text of Romanus Pontifex reads: "We weighing all and singular the premises with due meditation, and noting that since we had formerly by other letters of ours granted among other things free and ample faculty to the aforesaid King Alfonso—to invade, search out, capture, vanquish, and subdue all Saracens and pagans whatsoever, and other enemies of Christ wheresoever placed, and the kingdoms, dukedoms, principalities, dominions, possessions, and all movable and immovable goods whatsoever held and possessed by them and to reduce their persons to perpetual slavery, and to apply and appropriate to himself and his successors the kingdoms, dukedoms, counties, principalities, dominions, possessions, and goods, and to convert them to his and their use and profit—by having secured the said faculty, the said King Alfonso, or, by his authority, the aforesaid infante, justly and lawfully has acquired and possessed, and doth possess, these islands, lands, harbors, and seas, and they do of right belong and pertain to the said King Alfonso and his successors." "Papal Bull Dum Diversas, 18 June, 1452," Doctrine of Discovery, http://www.doctrineofdiscovery.org/dumdiversas.htm.

15. Spanish colonial law included a "charter for conquest" called the "Requerimiento," which was an order to Indigenous peoples to "acknowledge the church as the ruler and superior of the whole world, and the high priest called Pope. . . . But if you do not do this . . . we shall forcefully enter your country and shall make war against you in all ways and manners that we can, and shall subject to the yoke and obedience of the church." Naturally, it was read in a language the Indians couldn't understand.

16. "Papal Bull Dum Diversas, 14 June, 1452," The Doctrine of Discovery, http://www.doctrineofdiscovery.org/dumdiversas.htm. The doctrine of discovery has had far-reaching implications for Indigenous peoples internationally and, as reflected in the website Doctrineofdiscovery.org, there is now a global movement that seeks to have the Catholic Church rescind the papal bulls that are the foundation of the doctrine.

17. Quoted in Newcomb, *Pagans in the Promised Land*, 92.

18. See Robert A. Williams Jr., *Like a Loaded Weapon: The Rehnquist Court, Indian Rights, and the Legal History of Racism in America* (Minneapolis: University of Minnesota Press, 2005).

19. David E. Wilkins and K. Tsianina Lomawaima, *Uneven Ground: American Indian Sovereignty and Federal Law* (Norman: University of Oklahoma Press, 2001), 12.

20. According to the website Abolishcolumbusday.com, Italian immigrants celebrated Columbus Day as a holiday in San Francisco and New York in the 1860s. "Columbus Day Timeline," Abolish Columbus Day, http://www .abolishcolumbusday.com/columbus-day-timeline.html.

21. Hawaii State Legislature, http://www.capitol.hawaii.gov/hrscurrent/vol01 _ch0001-0042f/HRS0008/HRS_0008-0001_0005.htm.

22. "Get Involved," Abolish Columbus Day, http://www.abolishcolumbusday .com/get-involved.html.

23. Jessica Carro, "Do Other Countries Celebrate Columbus Day?," Indian Country Today Media Network, October 8, 2014, http://indiancountry todaymedianetwork.com/2014/10/08/do-other-countries-celebrate -columbus-day. The author notes that there is no such day of honoring of Columbus in Italy, and Spain acknowledges Fiesta Nacional (National Day) or El Día de la Hispanidad.

MYTH 4: "THANKSGIVING PROVES THE INDIANS WELCOMED THE PILGRIMS"

1. John S. Marr and John T. Cathey, "New Hypothesis for Cause of Epidemic Among Native Americans, New England, 1616–1619," *Emerging Infectious Diseases Journal* 16, no. 2 (February 2010), doi: 10.3201/eid1602.090276, http://wwwnc.cdc.gov/eid/article/16/2/09-0276_article.

2. Quoting Neal Salisbury, Marr and Cathey, ibid., say that between twenty-one thousand and twenty-four thousand is reasonable, while literature from the Plimoth Plantation museum gives a figure of between fifty thousand and one hundred thousand.

3. Quoted in James Loewen, *Lies My Teacher Told Me: Everything Your American History Textbook Got Wrong* (New York: Touchstone, 1995), 91. Historians believe that the robberies were from homes of the Nauset people, enemies of the English. Massasoit had agreed to intervene to settle the dispute, but it is unclear that recompense was adequately made.

4. Marr and Cathey, "New Hypothesis for Cause of Epidemic."

5. John H. Humins, "Squanto and Massasoit: A Struggle for Power," *New England Quarterly* 60, no. 1 (March 1987): 54–70.

6. Alden T. Vaughan, *New England Frontier: Puritans and Indians, 1620–1675* (Norman: University of Oklahoma Press, 1995), 70. Humins, "Squanto and Massasoit," notes that Massasoit's alliance was strongly opposed by some of the other sachems of the confederation.

7. Humins, "Squanto and Massasoit."

8. "Primary Sources for 'The First Thanksgiving' at Plymouth," Pilgrim Hall Museum, http://www.pilgrimhallmuseum.org/pdf/TG_What_Happened _in_1621.pdf.

9. On Indigenous relationships of reciprocity and ceremonials, see, generally, Gregory Cajete, *Native Science: Natural Laws of Interdependence* (Santa Fe: Clear Light Publishers, 2000).

10. "Primary Sources for 'The First Thanksgiving' at Plymouth" ("in modern spelling").

11. Gale Courey Toensing, "What Really Happened at the First Thanksgiving?," Indian Country Today Media Network, November 23, 2012, http://indian countrytodaymedianetwork.com/2012/11/23/what-really-happened-first -thanksgiving-wampanoag-side-tale-and-whats-done-today-145807.

12. The account also regularly refers to the colonists' Indian allies as "savages," implying an underlying view of them as inherently inferior.

13. Humins, "Squanto and Massasoit."

14. Nathaniel Philbrick, *Mayflower: A Story of Community, Courage, and War* (New York: Viking, 2006), 138.

MYTH 5: "INDIANS WERE SAVAGE AND WARLIKE"

1. "Savage," *Online Etymology Dictionary*, http://www.etymonline.com/.

2. This is confirmed in the language of various papal bulls that divided the lands of the "New World" among the Christian nations of Europe before the lands were even "discovered."

3. "Barbarian," *New World Encyclopedia*, http://www.newworldencyclopedia .org/entry/Barbarian.

4. "Civilization, Barbarism, Savagery," *Berkshire Encyclopedia of World History*, vol. 1, ed. William H. McNeill (Great Barrington, MA: Berkshire Publishing Group, 2005), 359.

5. Quoted in ibid.

6. Eve Tuck and K. Wayne Yang advance a model of colonization and decolonization that depicts the various ways settlers evade responsibility for the base of oppression their societies are built upon. These evasions constitute what they call "settler moves to innocence." Eve Tuck and K. Wayne Yang, "Decolonization Is Not a Metaphor," *Decolonization: Indigeneity, Education, and Society* 1, no. 1 (2012): 1–40, http://decolonization.org/index.php/des /article/view/18630/15554.

7. "Native American Warfare in the East: Mourning Wars," Encyclopedia.com, http://www.encyclopedia.com/doc/1G2-2536600186.html.

8. These practices, while not fully understood, fit within Indigenous cultural norms that tested bravery while also cementing group cohesion and

demonstrating Iroquois superiority over enemies. Daniel K. Richter, "War and Culture: The Iroquois Experience," *William and Mary Quarterly*, Third Series, 40, no. 4 (October 1983): 532–34.

9. Ibid., 528.

10. Ibid., 529.

11. Douglas Bamforth, "Indigenous People, Indigenous Violence: Precontact Warfare on the North American Great Plains," *Man*, New Series, 29, no. 1 (March 1994).

12. See, for example, James. F. Brooks, *Captives and Cousins: Slavery, Kinship, and Community in the Southwest Borderlands* (Chapel Hill: University of North Carolina Press, 2002).

13. Ned Blackhawk, *Violence over the Land: Indians and Empires in the Early American West* (Cambridge, MA: Harvard University Press, 2006).

14. Sibylle Scheipers, *Unlawful Combatants: A Genealogy of the Irregular Fighter* (New York: Oxford University Press, 2015), 33–36.

15. Ibid., 36.

16. John Grenier, *The First Way of War: American War Making on the Frontier, 1607–1814* (Cambridge, UK: Cambridge University Press, 2005), 10.

17. Roxanne Dunbar-Ortiz, *An Indigenous Peoples' History of the United States* (Boston: Beacon Press, 2014), 60.

18. Ibid., 61.

19. Philbrick, *Mayflower*, 179.

20. "Native American Warfare in the East: Mourning Wars."

21. Ibid.

22. Blackhawk, *Violence over the Land*, 2.

MYTH 6: "INDIANS SHOULD MOVE ON AND FORGET THE PAST"

1. Dunbar-Ortiz, *An Indigenous Peoples' History of the United States*, 6.

2. The phrase is widely attributed to John O'Sullivan, a newspaper editor who wrote in 1845 that it was "our manifest destiny to overspread the continent allotted by Providence for the free development of our yearly multiplying millions." Published in *United States Magazine and Democratic Review* 17, no. 1 (July–August 1845); available at http://web.grinnell.edu/courses/HIS/f01/HIS202-01/Documents/OSullivan.html.

3. Legal scholar Lindsay G. Robertson demonstrated the fraud and collusion in *M'Intosh* in his *Conquest by Law: How the Discovery of America Dispossessed Indigenous Peoples of Their Lands* (London: Oxford University Press, 2005). The book is a remarkable study made possible after previously unknown archives were discovered by the author in the 1990s.

4. Supreme Court Justice Clarence Thomas in *United States v. Lara* (2004), quoted in Williams, *Like a Loaded Weapon*, 158–60.

5. Quoted in Newcomb, *Pagans in the Promised Land*, 100.

6. Robertson, *Conquest by Law*, xiii.

7. David E. Wilkins, *American Indian Politics and the American Political System* (Lanham, MD: Rowman and Littlefield, 2002), 114.

8. Colleen O'Neill, "Rethinking Modernity and the Discourse of Development in American Indian History, an Introduction," in *Native Pathways: American Indian Culture and Economic Development in the 20th Century*, ed. Brian Hosmer and Colleen O'Neill (Boulder: University Press of Colorado, 2004), 1–26.

9. Ibid., 14.

10. Scott Lyons, "Actually Existing Indian Nations: Modernity, Diversity, and the Future of the Native American Studies," *American Indian Quarterly* 35, no. 3 (Summer 2011): 294–312.

11. Ibid., 305.

12. Dennis F. Kelley, "Ancient Traditions, Modern Constructions: Innovation, Continuity, and Spirituality on the Powwow Trail," *Journal for the Study of Religions and Ideologies* 11, no. 33 (Winter 2012): 122.

13. Ibid., 116. Kelley notes that he prefers the musical term "reprise" to "revitalization," "revival," "resuscitation," and others because it "alludes to the articulation of an earlier theme whose basic elements remain present throughout."

MYTH 7: "EUROPEANS BROUGHT CIVILIZATION TO THE BACKWARD INDIANS"

1. Vine Deloria Jr., *Custer Died for Your Sins: An Indian Manifesto* (Norman: University of Oklahoma Press, 1969), 81.

2. Ibid., 93.

3. Robert F. Berkhofer, *The White Man's Indian: Images of the American Indian from Columbus to the Present* (New York: Random House, 1978).

4. Reginald Horsman, "Scientific Racism and the American Indian in the Mid-Nineteenth Century," *American Quarterly* 27, no. 2 (May 1975): 152–68.

5. Ibid., 152.

6. Quoted in Berkhofer, *The White Man's Indian*, 58–59.

7. G. Reginald Daniel, "Either Black or White: Race, Modernity, and the Law of the Excluded Middle," in *Racial Thinking in the United States: Uncompleted Independence*, ed. Paul R. Spickard and G. Reginald Daniel (Notre Dame, IN: University of Notre Dame Press, 2004), 31.

8. The belief in the improvability of the Indian race was not ubiquitous. For decades throughout the mid-nineteenth century, scientific and political debates centered on whether or not Indian savagery could be overcome through environment (adopting the ways of European civilization) or

through Indian interbreeding with whites, and thus their eventual disappearance. See Horsman, "Scientific Racism."

9. A new generation of scholarship is overturning the mythic settler stereotype of Indians as wandering bands of nomads. A large percentage of Fourth World peoples on the North American continent in fact practiced some form of agriculture (many quite advanced) in addition to gathering, hunting game, and fishing for subsistence. Contrary to the popular historic myths that they "roamed" over a virgin landscape, many Indigenous nations practiced extensive land management techniques. They also exercised complex forms of governance that included ancient practices of diplomacy that informed their centuries-long treaty relationships with France, Spain, England, and, later, the United States.

10. Williams, *Like a Loaded Weapon*, xxv.

MYTH 8: "THE UNITED STATES DID NOT HAVE A POLICY OF GENOCIDE"

1. Vincent Schilling, "History Professor Denies Native Genocide: Native Student Disagreed, Then Says Professor Expelled Her From Course," Indian Country Today Media Network, September 6, 2015, https://indiancountry todaymedianetwork.com/2015/09/06/history-professor-denies-native -genocide-native-student-disagrees-gets-expelled-course.

2. Colleen Flaherty, "Not Up for Debate?," *Inside Higher Ed*, September 15, 2015, https://www.insidehighered.com/news/2015/09/15/sacramento-state -student-says-she-was-kicked-out-class-arguing-native-americans-were.

3. See Dunbar-Ortiz, *An Indigenous Peoples' History of the United States*, for more on the counterinsurgency warfare against Natives.

4. Lyman H. Legters, "The American Genocide," *Policy Studies Journal* 16, no. 4 (Summer 1988).

5. A. Dirk Moses, "Moving the Genocide Debate Beyond the History Wars," *Australian Journal of Politics and History* 54, no. 2 (2008): 248–70.

6. Benjamin Madley, "Reexamining the American Genocide Debate: Meaning, Historiography, and New Methods," *American Historical Review* 120, no. 1 (February 2015): 98–139.

7. "The Legal Definition of Genocide," Prevent Genocide International, http:// www.preventgenocide.org/genocide/officialtext-printerfriendly.htm.

8. The federal government mandated attendance in residential boarding schools under the Dawes Act as part of its civilizing mission. Regarding adoption, throughout the nineteenth and twentieth centuries so many Indian children were removed from their homes and adopted out into white homes (as much as 30 percent of all Native children) that the Indian Child Welfare Act was passed in 1978 to give priority to tribal

nations in adoption cases, a law that is currently under attack by the religious right.

9. Brendan C. Lindsay, *Murder State: California's Native American Genocide, 1846–1873* (Lincoln: University of Nebraska Press, 2014), 17.

10. Benjamin Madley, "'Unholy Traffic in Human Blood and Souls': Systems of California Indian Servitude Under U.S. Rule," *Pacific Historical Review* 83, no. 4 (2014): 626–67.

11. Lindsay, *Murder State*, 156.

12. Ibid., 22.

13. Ibid., 25–26.

14. The ideology of extermination was declared by then governor Peter Hardeman Burnett, who, in an 1851 speech to the legislature, stated, "A war of extermination will continue to be waged between the two races until the Indian race becomes extinct, must be expected." Quoted in "Governor Brown Issues Proclamation Declaring Native American Day," September 27, 2013, http://gov.ca.gov/news.php?id=18213. Lindsay identifies a journal article in 1977 that appears to be the first explicit reference to California Indian genocide in the scholarly literature. Lindsay, *Murder State*, 5.

15. Lindsay, *Murder State*, 26.

16. Ibid., x.

17. Nicole Winfield, "Vatican Defends Canonization of Junipero Serra, Controversial Hispanic Evangelizer," *Huffington Post*, April 20, 2015, http://www.huffingtonpost.com/2015/04/20/vatican-junipero-serra_n _7099656.html.

18. Jeremy Leaming, "Mission Unconstitutional: Congress Considers $10-Million Grant for California Mission Churches," *Church and State*, March 2004, https://www.au.org/church-state/march-2004-church-state /featured/mission-unconstitutional.

19. Robert Archibald, "Indian Labor at the California Missions: Slavery or Salvation," *Journal of San Diego History* 24, no. 2 (Spring 1978); San Diego History Center Online, http://www.sandiegohistory.org/journal/78spring /labor.htm.

20. Elias Castillo, "About the Book," http://www.eliasacastillo.net/about.html. According to Castillo and other scholars, some sixty-two thousand Indians died as a result of disease, overwork, and malnutrition in the mission system between 1769 and 1833.

21. The petition was created by a California Indian woman named Norma Flores under the alias of Toypurina Carac, a tribute to a twenty-four-year-old Tongva medicine woman who was known for inspiring a rebellion at San Gabriel Mission in 1785.

22. David Gibson, "Pope Francis Canonizes, and Defends, Controversial Spanish Missionary," Religion News Service, September 23, 2015, http://www .religionnews.com/2015/09/23/pope-francis-canonizes-defends -controversial-spanish-missionary-junipero-serra.

MYTH 9: "US PRESIDENTS WERE BENEVOLENT OR AT LEAST FAIR-MINDED TOWARD INDIANS"

1. Levi Rickert, "US Presidents in Their Own Words Concerning American Indians," Native News Online, February 16, 2015, http://nativenewsonline .net/currents/us-presidents-words-concerning-american-indians.
2. Woody Holton, *Unruly Americans and the Origins of the Constitution* (New York: Hill and Wang, 2007), 14.
3. Washington and Sullivan quoted in Richard Drinnon, *Facing West: The Metaphysics of Indian-Hating and Empire-Building* (Minneapolis: University of Minnesota Press, 1980), 331.
4. Grenier, *The First Way of War*, 170–72.
5. Wilma Mankiller and Michael Wallis, *Mankiller: A Chief and Her People* (New York: St. Martin's Press, 1993), 51.
6. For a survey of the role of US presidents, see Wilkins, *American Indian Politics and the American Political System*, 83–92. From the Department of Defense website: "The Department of Defense is America's oldest and largest government agency. With our military tracing its roots back to pre-Revolutionary times, the Department of Defense has grown and evolved with our nation. . . . The Army, Navy, and Marine Corps were established in 1775, in concurrence with the American Revolution." "About the Department of Defense," US Department of Defense, http://www.defense.gov /About-DoD. "Department of Defense" was the name created in 1947. Before that, from the founding of the United States, it was called the Department of War, which is not mentioned on the DoD website.
7. Wilkins, *American Indian Politics and the American Political System*, 67, 83; Vine Deloria Jr., "Congress in Its Wisdom: The Course of Indian Legislation," in *The Aggressions of Civilization: Federal Indian Policy Since the 1880s*, ed. Sandra L. Cadwalader and Vine Deloria Jr. (Philadelphia: Temple University Press, 1984), 106–7.

MYTH 10: "THE ONLY REAL INDIANS ARE FULL-BLOODS, AND THEY ARE DYING OFF"

1. In the short film on Indian identity by Jonathan Tomhave titled *Half of Anything*, the acclaimed writer Sherman Alexie elaborates on how his appearance can make him ambiguous depending on the length of his hair, how tan his skin is, and where he is. "Indian identity has almost exclusively become something physical, the way you look or dress or the way you act. It's very surface," he says. Talking about being a writer who lives away from

his home on the Spokane reservation, he reveals that "with short hair [and paler skin from not being in the sun] I blend into Seattle. I could be Asian, I could be Mexican, I could be Middle Eastern, I could be Italian. . . . [I] could be half of anything."

2. Based on a study of Navajo identity, Sam Pack rejects the blood = culture paradigm, arguing that recent research confirms no causal relationship between blood quantum and cultural authenticity. But it is so pervasive that even in Native communities this "blood hegemony" has become internalized, so that race mixing is directly associated with cultural loss. Sam Pack, "What Is a Real Indian? The Interminable Debate of Cultural Authenticity," *AlterNative: An International Journal of Indigenous Scholarship* 8, no. 2 (2012): 176–88.

3. Ryan W. Schmidt, "American Indian Identity and Blood Quantum in the 21st Century: A Critical Review," *Journal of Anthropology* (2011), doi:10.1155/2011/549521. For more on the origins of blood as a conveyor of identity and culture, see Melissa L. Meyer, "American Indian Blood Quantum Requirements: Blood Is Thicker Than Family," in *Over the Edge: Remapping the American West*, ed. V. J. Matsumoto and B. Allmendinger (Berkeley: University of California Press, 1999), 231–49; and Melissa L. Meyer, *Thicker Than Water: The Origins of Blood as Symbol and Ritual* (New York: Routledge, 2005).

4. Schmidt, "American Indian Identity and Blood Quantum," 5.

5. Alexandra Harmon, "Tribal Enrollment Councils: Lessons on Law and Indian Identity," *Western Historical Quarterly* 32 (2001): 175–200.

6. For more on the remaking of modern Indian nations, see Vine Deloria Jr. and Clifford M. Lytle, *The Nations Within: The Past and Future of American Indian Sovereignty* (Austin: University of Texas Press, 1984).

7. Harmon's Colville study, for example, shows how Indian agents attempted to convince tribal councils that regulating the allotment distributions by excluding people with low blood quantum would protect the economic interests of Indians already on the roll. Harmon, "Tribal Enrollment Councils," 179.

8. The preeminent example of the parentage conundrum, ironically, is the Supreme Court decision that upholds tribal sovereignty in membership matters, *Santa Clara Pueblo v. Martinez* (1978). Julia Martinez, a member of Santa Clara Pueblo, sued the tribe for not enrolling her half-Navajo children because Santa Clara's laws affirm enrollment only through the father. In other words, as legal scholars have observed in this problematic decision, tribal sovereignty trumped equal protection under the law.

9. See Jessica Bardill, "Tribal Enrollment and Genetic Testing," National Congress of American Indians, American Indian & Alaska Native Genetics

Resource Center, n.d., http://genetics.ncai.org/tribal-enrollment-and
-genetic-testing.cfm.

10. For detailed analyses of genetic testing and American Indian heritage, see
Kim Tallbear's award-winning book *Native American DNA: Tribal Belonging
and the False Promise of Genetic Science* (Minneapolis: University of Minnesota Press, 2013).

11. Jessica Bardill, "Tribal Sovereignty and Enrollment Determinations,"
National Congress of American Indians, American Indian & Alaska Native
Genetics Resource Center, n.d., http://genetics.ncai.org/tribal-sovereignty
-and-enrollment-determinations.cfm.

12. For more on indigeneity, kinship, and authenticity, see Eva Marie Gar-
routte, *Real Indians: Identity and the Survival of Native America* (Berkeley:
University of California Press, 2003); Circe Sturm, *Blood Politics: Race, Culture, and Identity in the Cherokee Nation of Oklahoma* (Berkeley: University of
California Press, 2002); and Joanne Barker, *Native Acts: Law, Recognition,
and Cultural Authenticity* (Durham, NC: Duke University Press, 2011).

MYTH 11: "THE UNITED STATES GAVE INDIANS THEIR RESERVATIONS"

1. We borrow the phrase "benevolent supremacy" from Melani McCalister's
book *Epic Encounters: Culture, Media, and U.S. Interests in the Middle East
Since 1945* (Berkeley: University of California Press, 2005), where "benevolent supremacy" describes a pattern of behaviors and policies the United
States adopted to dominate the Middle East in order to secure access to its
oil resources. It also serves as a good descriptor for a much older pattern of
US paternalism in its dealings with Indigenous peoples in order to secure
access to land and other resources. Benevolent supremacy can be thought
of as a way of enacting a settler colonialism system while downplaying its
inherent injustice and masking the contradictions such a system poses in a
democratic society.

2. "Frequently Asked Questions," Bureau of Indian Affairs, US Department of
the Interior, http://www.bia.gov/FAQs. In a very real sense Native nations
do not even own the titles to their lands in the same way that the title is
owned in fee simple. It is often referred to as "aboriginal title."

3. For more on capitalism and political economy in Indian country, see Dina
Gilio-Whitaker, "Fourth World Nations' Collision with Capitalism in the
United States," *Fourth World Journal* 13, no. 2 (2014): 1–20.

4. Donald L. Fixico notes that while federal Indian policy between 1920 and
1945 did not involve deliberate attempts to terminate or relocate Native
communities, they were still pressured to approve organizations under
the Indian Reorganization Act in order to receive federal assistance. See

Fixico, *Termination and Relocation: Federal Indian Policy, 1945–1960* (Albuquerque: University of New Mexico Press, 1986).

5. Fixico argues that termination and relocation are erroneously attributed to the Eisenhower administration. In reality, he says, the seeds of both policies were sown during the Truman administration. Ibid., 183.

6. Ibid.

7. Ibid.

8. See Laurie Arnold, *Bartering with the Bones of Their Dead: The Colville Confederated Tribes and Termination* (Seattle: University of Washington Press, 2012). For a brief synopsis of the book and interview with the author, see Dina Gilio-Whitaker, "Native History: The Epic Termination Battle on the Colville Indian Reservation," Indian Country Today Media Network, September 2, 2015, http://indiancountrytodaymedianetwork. com/2015/09/02/native-history-epic-termination-battle-colville-indian -reservation-161379. The Colville termination story demonstrates how many Indian people in the 1950s and 1960s viewed themselves (and wanted to be viewed) as modern people, capable of economic self-sufficiency, while also firmly rooted in their Native identities. In addition they believed that the Bureau of Indian Affairs was a malevolent force that inhibited their ability to be self-sufficient.

9. Renya K. Ramirez, *Native Hubs: Culture, Community, and Belonging in Silicon Valley and Beyond* (Durham, NC: Duke University Press, 2007), notes that these Native spaces and activities are virtual as well and occur through reading tribal newspapers and on the Internet. Indeed, social media have become irreplaceable as an organizing tool, as is visible in the rise of the Idle No More movement, discussed in myth 21.

10. Ibid., 12.

11. Ibid.

MYTH 12: "INDIANS ARE WARDS OF THE STATE"

1. Gale Courey Toensing, "Are American Indian Nations 'Wards of the Federal Government'?," Indian Country Today Media Network, December 19, 2014, http://indiancountrytodaymedianetwork.com/2014/12/19/are -american-indian-nations-wards-federal-government-158375.

2. Ibid.

3. See Dina Gilio-Whitaker, "Resolution Copper: 6 Egregious Examples of Parent Rio Tinto's Rights Violations Worldwide," Indian Country Today Media Network, July 23, 2015, http://indiancountrytodaymedianetwork .com/2015/07/23/resolution-copper-6-egregious-examples-parent -rio-tintos-rights-violations-worldwide.

4. Gosar's "wards of the government" statement was in line with a pattern of attacks on Indian country that characterized the 114th Congress. See Gale Courey Toensing, "Rep. Don Young Is Leading an Assault on Native Rights," Indian Country Today Media Network, May 27, 2015, http://indiancountrytodaymedianetwork.com/2015/05/27/rep-don-young-leading-assault-native-rights-160494.
5. Wilkins and Lomawaima, *Uneven Ground*, 109.
6. Toensing, "Are American Indian Nations 'Wards of the Federal Government'?"
7. See Wilkins and Lomawaima, *Uneven Ground*, chapter 3, for an in-depth discussion of the plenary power doctrine.
8. Ibid., 111.
9. Ibid., 100; Laurence M. Hauptman, "Congress, Plenary Power, and the American Indian, 1872–1992," in *Exiled in the Land of the Free: Democracy, Indian Nations, and the U.S. Constitution*, ed. Oren Lyons et al. (Santa Fe: Clear Light Publishers, 1992), 317–36.
10. Wilkins and Lomawaima, *Uneven Ground*, 66.
11. This view is evidenced in the fifteen-year-long Cobell lawsuit that resulted in the Claims Settlement Act of 2010.

MYTH 13: "SPORTS MASCOTS HONOR NATIVE AMERICANS"
1. Leila Atassi, "Cleveland Councilman Zack Reed Says Chief Wahoo Is the 'Red Sambo,' Calls for City to Ban Logo from Public Spaces," Cleveland.com, April 10, 2014, http://www.cleveland.com/cityhall/index.ssf/2014/04/cleveland_councilman_zack_reed_11.html.
2. James O. Young, *Cultural Appropriation and the Arts* (Malden, MA: Blackwell, 2010), 5.
3. Philip Deloria, *Playing Indian* (New Haven, CT: Yale University Press, 1998). The Boston Tea Party is remembered in US history as the catalyst for the Revolutionary War. Protesting England's Tea Act, the Sons of Liberty rebel group, disguised as Indians, dumped shipping containers of tea into Boston Harbor.
4. The possible exception would be when non-Native people participate in Native cultural events, such as dancing in powwows in full regalia. In a case like this, many (though not all) Native people do not consider such participation offensive, as long as established protocols are being followed appropriately and respectfully.
5. See Jason Edward Black, "The 'Mascotting' of Native America: Construction, Commodity, and Assimilation," *American Indian Quarterly* 26, no. 4 (Autumn 2002): 605–22.

6. "Ending the Legacy of Racism in Sports and the Era of Harmful 'Indian' Sports Mascots," National Congress of American Indians, October 2013, http://www.ncai.org/resources/ncai-publications/Ending_the_Legacy_of _Racism.pdf.

7. In 2005 the NCAA established a policy requiring colleges and universities with American Indian mascots and logos not to display those images during NCAA-sponsored events. If they did, they would be ineligible to host NCAA championships starting in 2006.

8. "Ending the Legacy of Racism in Sports," 5.

9. Ibid., 5.

10. Ibid., 10.

11. Ibid., 14.

12. Michael Taylor, "The Salamanca Warriors: A Case Study of an 'Exception to the Rule,'" *Journal of Anthropological Research* 67, no. 2 (Summer 2011): 245–65.

13. Kristen Dorsey, "Decolonizing the Runway," *Cultural Survival Quarterly* 37, no. 2 (June 2013): 10–11.

14. Ibid.

15. The appropriation of feather headdresses is offensive because in Plains Indian cultures such regalia are considered sacred (especially since most of the time they are made with eagle feathers), and the right to wear one must be earned. Furthermore, by and large only men are granted the right to wear them, so when non-Native women wear them as costume it constitutes a double offense.

16. Susan Scafidi, "When Native American Appropriation Is Appropriate," *Time*, June 6, 2014, http://time.com/2840461/pharrell-native-american -headdress.

17. Ellen J. Staurowsky, "'You Know, We Are All Indian': Exploring White Power and Privilege in Reactions to the NCAA Native American Mascot Policy," *Journal of Sport & Social Issues* 31, no. 1 (February 2007): 62.

MYTH 14: "NATIVE AMERICAN CULTURE BELONGS TO ALL AMERICANS"

1. Matt Stroud, "Self-Help Author Imprisoned for Sweat Lodge Deaths Is Making a Comeback," *Bloomberg Business*, March 3, 2015, http://www .bloomberg.com/news/articles/2015-03-03/self-help-author-imprisoned -for-sweat-lodge-deaths-is-making-a-comeback.

2. "Self-Help Shamster Behind Sweat-Lodge Homicides Released from Prison," Indian Country Today Media Network, July 13, 2013, http:// indiancountrytodaymedianetwork.com/2013/07/13/james-arthur-ray -released-prison-no-not-guy-who-killed-mlk-150407.

3. Takatoka and Friends, "Sweat Lodge Deaths Attributed to Greed and Ignorance," Manataka American Indian Council, http://www.manataka.org
   /page1108.html.
4. "Native History: A Non-Traditional Sweat Leads to Three Deaths," Indian
   Country Today Media Network, October 8, 2013. http://indiancountry
   todaymedianetwork.com/2013/10/08/native-history-non-traditional
   -sweat-leads-tragedy-151634.
5. Valerie Taliman, "Selling the Sacred," Indian Country Today Media Network, October 14, 2009, http://indiancountrytodaymedianetwork.com
   /opinion/selling-the-sacred-15597.
6. Suzanne Owen, *The Appropriation of Native American Spirituality* (New York:
   Continuum, 2008), 2.
7. Ibid., 3.
8. Rayna Green, "The Tribe Called Wannabee: Playing Indian in America and
   Europe," *Folklore* 99, no. 1 (1988): 30–55.
9. Lisa Aldred, "Plastic Shamans and Astroturf Sun Dances: New Age Commercialization of Native American Spirituality," *American Indian Quarterly*
   24, no. 3 (Summer 2000): 330–31.
10. According to Native scholar Dr. Dean Chavers, Carlos Castaneda's books
    (which garnered him a PhD from the University of California at Los
    Angeles) were found to be so fraudulent that the degree was rescinded
    many years later. Chavers notes it's the only case he's ever heard of where a
    degree was taken back. "The Fake Carlos Castaneda," Indian Country Today
    Media Network, March 24, 2011, http://indiancountrytodaymedianetwork
    .com/2011/03/24/fake-carlos-castaneda-24168.
11. Aldred, "Plastic Shamans and Astroturf Sun Dances," 336–37.
12. Ibid., 336, quoting plastic shaman/poet Gary Snyder.
13. For an expanded discussion on universality, spiritual appropriation,
    and its relationship to the "pioneer spirit," see Wendy Rose, "The Great
    Pretenders: Further Reflections on Whiteshamanism," in *Native American
    Voices: A Reader*, ed. Susan Lobo and Steve Talbot (Upper Saddle River, NJ:
    Prentice-Hall, 2001), 330–43.
14. This explains the high level of secrecy with which Pueblo and Hopi peoples
    guard their kiva ceremonies and even languages.
15. It is not a little ironic that Iron Eyes Cody turned out to be not Native
    American at all but the son of Sicilian immigrants.
16. Quoted in Noël Sturgeon, *Environmentalism in Popular Culture: Gender,
    Race, Sexuality, and the Politics of the Natural* (Tucson: University of Arizona
    Press, 2009), 78–79.
17. Staurowsky, "'You Know, We Are All Indian,'" 61–67.

18. Smith held a dual appointment in the Department of Women's Studies and the Native American Studies program within the Department of American Culture, of which she was the interim chair. Her bid for tenure was supported by the American Culture Department while it was denied by Women's Studies. It was unclear why the tenure bid was declined.

19. See Dean Chavers, "5 Fake Indians: Checking a Box Doesn't Make You Native," Indian Country Today Media Network, October 15, 2014, http://indiancountrytodaymedianetwork.com/2014/10/15/5-fake-indians-checking-box-doesnt-make-you-native-157179?page=0%2C2.

20. Deloria, *Playing Indian*.

21. Tuck and Yang, "Decolonization Is Not a Metaphor," 10.

22. Ibid., 28, 35.

MYTH 15: "MOST INDIANS ARE ON GOVERNMENT WELFARE"

1. "About Us," Indian Health Service, https://www.ihs.gov/aboutihs.

2. "Basis for Health Services," Indian Health Service, https://www.ihs.gov/newsroom/factsheets/basisforhealthservices.

3. "IHS Year 2014 Profile," Indian Health Service, https://www.ihs.gov/newsroom/index.cfm/factsheets/ihsyear2014profile.

4. "Tribal Colleges," American Indian College Fund, http://www.collegefund.org/content/tribal_colleges.

5. In a personal conversation with American Indian College Fund personnel, we were told that the applications are subjected to a scoring process, where the highest-scoring applications are awarded scholarships.

6. In 2011 a lawsuit brought by the Rincon Band of Luiseño Indians found that Schwarzenegger had illegally taxed them and failed to negotiate their compacts in good faith. See Bo Mazzetti, "How Arnold Schwarzenegger Violated Tribal Sovereignty," Indian Country Today Media Network, September 21, 2011, http://indiancountrytodaymedianetwork.com/2011/09/21/how-arnold-schwarzenegger-violated-tribal-sovereignty.

7. Ernest L. Stevens, "Indian Gaming: Misconception vs. Fact," Indian Gaming, http://www.indiangaming.com/istore/May15_Stevens.pdf.

8. Per capita payments are payments distributed to tribal members from income generated by tribal businesses.

9. Gale Courey Toensing, "IRS Harassing Tribes with Audits, Threatening Sovereignty," Indian Country Today Media Network, July 1, 2013, http://indiancountrytodaymedianetwork.com/2013/07/01/irs-harassing-tribes-audits-threatening-sovereignty-150211.

10. Rob Capriccioso, "Tribes Say IRS Moves to Tax Tribal Per Capita Payments; Congress Investigates," Indian Country Today Media Network, September

19, 2012, http://indiancountrytodaymedianetwork.com/2012/09/19/tribes-say-irs-moves-tax-tribal-capita-payments-congress-investigates-134775.

11. Wendy Pearson, Will Micklin, and Holly Easterling, *Indian Tribal Governments: Report on the General Welfare Doctrine as Applied to Indian Tribal Governments and Their Members* (Washington, DC: Advisory Committee on Tax Exempt and Government Entities, 2012), http://www.ncai.org/IRS_Advisory_Committee_on_Tax_Exempt_Entities_-_2012_Report.pdf.

12. "Support for the Tribal General Welfare Exclusion Act of 2013," National Congress of American Indians Resolution #TUL-13–032, http://www.ncai.org/resources/resolutions/support-for-the-tribal-general-welfare-exclusion-act-of-2013-pending-in-congress.

13. After its passage, Dina wrote an editorial questioning the nobility of the act. See Dina Gilio-Whitaker, "Tribal General Welfare Exclusion Act: Landmark Legislation or Hollow Victory?," Indian Country Today Media Network, November 21, 2014, http://indiancountrytodaymedianetwork.com/2014/11/21/tribal-general-welfare-exclusion-act-landmark-legislation-or-hollow-victory.

14. *Federal Funding to Indian Nations and Communities Tax Payments to the United States: A Preliminary Assessment* (Olympia, WA: Center for World Indigenous Studies, 2013), i–ii.

15. Ibid., 2.

16. It seems important to note that under the Indian Claims Commission, no land was ever returned.

17. US Department of Justice, "Attorney General Holder and Secretary Salazar Announce $1 Billion Settlement of Tribal Trust Accounting and Management Lawsuits Filed by More Than 40 Tribes," press release, April 11, 2012, http://www.justice.gov/opa/pr/2012/April/12-ag-460.html.

18. Mary Hudetz, "Feds to Pay $940M to Settle Claims over Tribal Contracts," Associated Press, September 17, 2015, http://bigstory.ap.org/article/1c2cc0286f6f41d89d82613ee363ec2a/feds-pay-940m-settle-claims-over-tribal-contracts.

19. Jens Manuel Krogstad, "One-in-Four Native Americans and Alaska Natives Are Living in Poverty," Pew Research Center, June 13, 2014, http://www.pewresearch.org/fact-tank/2014/06/13/1-in-4-native-americans-and-alaska-natives-are-living-in-poverty.

MYTH 16: "INDIAN CASINOS MAKE THEM ALL RICH"

1. 2014 Tribal Gaming Revenues by Gaming Operation Revenue Range, National Indian Gaming Commission, http://www.nigc.gov/images/uploads/reports/2014GGRbyGamingOperationRevenueRange.pdf.

2. Harvard Project on American Indian Economic Development, *The State of the Native Nations: Conditions Under U.S. Policies of Self-Determination*, "draft manuscript January 2007," http://isites.harvard.edu/fs/docs/icb.topic177572 .files/SONN_Final_01_09_07.pdf.
3. Ibid.
4. Steve Tetrault, "After Growth, Indian Gaming Now 'Pretty Flat,'" *Las Vegas Review-Journal*, July 23, 2014, http://www.reviewjournal.com/business /casinos-gaming/after-growth-indian-gaming-now-pretty-flat.
5. Ibid.
6. Krogstad, "One-in-Four Native Americans and Alaska Natives Are Living in Poverty."
7. Celeste Lacroix, "High-Stakes Stereotypes: The Emergence of the 'Casino Indian' Trope in Television Depictions of Contemporary Native Americans," *Howard Journal of Communications* 22, no. 1 (2011): 3, 18.
8. Alexandra Harmon, *Rich Indians: Native People and the Problem of Wealth in American History* (Chapel Hill: University of North Carolina Press, 2010), 5.
9. Ibid., 3.
10. A 2011 court decision determined the illegality of Schwarzenegger's tactics. See Mazzetti, "How Arnold Schwarzenegger Violated Tribal Sovereignty."
11. Jeff Corntassel and Richard C. Witmer II, *Forced Federalism: Contemporary Challenges to Indigenous Nationhood* (Norman: University of Oklahoma Press, 2008), 29–30.
12. Jeffrey Hawkins, "Smoke Signals, Sitting Bulls, and Slot Machines: A New Stereotype of Native Americans?," *Multicultural Perspectives* 7, no. 3 (2005): 51–54.

MYTH 17: "INDIANS ARE ANTI-SCIENCE"

1. Jason Antrosio, "Earliest Americans, Battle of the Bones, Native American DNA," *Living Anthropologically*, July 12, 2012, http://www.living anthropologically.com/2012/07/12/earliest-americans-bones -anthropology.
2. Dienekes Pontikos, "Reconstructing the Origin of Native American Populations," *Dienekes Anthropology Blog*, July 11, 2012, http://dienekes.blogspot .com/2012/07/reconstructing-origin-of-native.html.
3. Razib Khan, "Native Americans Are Not Special Snowflakes," *Gene Expression* (*Discover* blog), http://blogs.discovermagazine.com/gnxp/2012/07 /native-americans-are-not-special-snowflakes/#.VkO1WfmrRGN.
4. The best example is the case of the Havasupai Indians who donated blood samples for a study on diabetes through Arizona State University in 1989. Without the tribe's consent, however, researchers used the DNA to conduct

other studies on schizophrenia, migration, and inbreeding, all of which are taboo subjects for the Havasupai. A bitter and long legal battle ensued, resulting in a $700,000 settlement being paid to the tribe in 2010 funds for a clinic and school—and the blood samples returned.

5. Cajete, *Native Science.*
6. Ibid., 140.
7. Ibid., 141.
8. Linda Barrington, "The Mississippians and Economic Development Before European Colonization," in *The Other Side of the Frontier: Economic Explorations into Native American History*, ed. Linda Barrington (Boulder, CO: Westview Press, 1999), 92.
9. Cajete, *Native Science*, 200.
10. Ramiro Matos Mendieta and José Barreiro, eds., *The Great Inka Road: Engineering an Empire* (Washington, DC: National Museum of the American Indian/Smithsonian Books, 2015).
11. "Native American Tomol," *Canoe and Kayak Magazine Online*, October 2, 2007, http://www.canoekayak.com/canoe/tomolcrossingchanelislands.
12. Blake Edgar, "The Polynesian Connection," *Archaeology* 58, no. 2 (March/April 2005): 42–45.
13. Blake De Pastino, "11,000-Year-Old Seafaring Indian Sites Discovered on California Island," *Western Digs*, January 6, 2014, http://westerndigs.org/11000-year-old-seafaring-indian-sites-discovered-on-california-island.
14. For more on Western versus Indigenous epistemologies and worldviews, see Linda Tuhiwai Smith, *Decolonizing Methodologies: Research and Indigenous Peoples*, 2nd ed. (London: Zed Books, 2012); Viola Cordova, *How It Is: The Native American Philosophy of V. F. Cordova*, ed. Kathleen Dean Moore, Kurt Peters, Ted Jojola, and Amber Lacy (Tucson: University of Arizona Press, 2007); Newcomb, *Pagans in the Promised Land*; and Norman K. Denzin, Yvonna S. Lincoln, and Linda Tuhiwai Smith, eds., *Handbook of Critical and Indigenous Methodologies* (Thousand Oaks, CA: Sage, 2008).
15. Daniel Gibson, "Native Scientists Taking Off," *Native Peoples*, November/December 2002, http://www.nativepeoples.com/Native-Peoples/November-December-2002/Native-Scientists-Taking-Off.
16. See "Project Overview: Why a Native American Science Curriculum?," Native American Science Curriculum, http://www.nativeamericanscience.org/about-us/overview.
17. *Generations of Knowledge*, Indigenous Education Institute, http://indigenousedu.org/wp/generations-of-knowledge-omsi.

MYTH 18: "INDIANS ARE NATURALLY PREDISPOSED TO ALCOHOLISM"

1. John W. Frank, Roland S. Moore, and Genevieve M. Ames, "Historical and Cultural Roots of Drinking Problems Among American Indians," *Public Health Then and Now* 90, no. 3 (March 2000): 344–51.

2. Don Coyhis and William L. White, "Alcohol Problems in Native America," *Alcoholism Treatment Quarterly* 20, nos. 3–4 (2002): 157–65, http://dx.doi .org/10.1300/J020v20n03_10.

3. See, for example, Fred Beauvais, "American Indians and Alcohol," *Spotlight on Special Populations* (National Institute on Alcohol Abuse and Alcoholism) 22, no. 4 (1998): 253–59.

4. Ibid.

5. Frank, Moore, and Ames, "Historical and Cultural Roots of Drinking Problems."

6. Beauvais, "American Indians and Alcohol."

7. Quoted in Coyhis and White, "Alcohol Problems in Native America."

8. Nancy Oestreich Lurie, "The World's Oldest On-Going Protest Demonstration: North American Indian Drinking Patterns," *Pacific Historical Review* 40, no. 3 (August 1971): 311–32, http://www.jstor.org/stable /3638360.

9. Frank, Moore, and Ames, "Historical and Cultural Roots of Drinking Problems."

10. Phillip A. May, "The Epidemiology of Alcohol Abuse Among American Indians: The Mythical and Real Properties," in Lobo and Talbot, eds., *Native American Voices*, 436–47.

11. Ibid., 438.

12. Ibid., 447.

13. Ibid., 440.

14. Eduardo Duran and Bonnie Duran, *Native American Postcolonial Psychology* (Albany: State University of New York Press, 1995).

15. Duran and Duran's criticism about medicalizing alcoholism (ibid., 112) includes the disease theory, which in their view is unnecessary and irrelevant.

16. Ibid., 100–101.

17. Ibid., 114.

18. Ibid., 103.

19. Historical trauma (also known as intergenerational trauma) can be thought of as a range of responses (including depression, post-traumatic stress disorder, and unresolved grief) to histories of genocide, forced acculturation, and cultural loss. It affects people on the personal, family, and societal levels.

20. Studies such as one from 2004 confirm the effects of discrimination and historical loss on alcohol abuse. Discriminatory acts serve as blatant reminders of ethnic cleansing and can trigger a sense of loss, for which alcohol likely serves as a way to numb reminders of that loss. Alcohol abuse may also signal self-destructive behavior as a manifestation of anger. See Les B. Whitbeck et al., "Discrimination, Historical Loss and Enculturation: Culturally Specific Risk and Resiliency Factors for Alcohol Abuse Among American Indians," *Journal of Studies on Alcohol* 65, no. 4 (July 2004): 409–18.

21. Duran and Duran, *Native American Postcolonial Psychology*, 126.

MYTH 19: "WHAT'S THE PROBLEM WITH THINKING OF INDIAN WOMEN AS PRINCESSES OR SQUAWS?"

1. For more on this binary stereotype, see Alma Garcia, *Contested Images: Women of Color in Popular Culture* (Lanham, MD: Altimira Press, 2012), 156–58.

2. Devon Abbott Mihesuah, *Indigenous American Women: Decolonization, Empowerment, Activism* (Lincoln: University of Nebraska Press, 2003), 7.

3. Garcia, *Contested Images*, 157.

4. National Museum of the American Indian, *Do All Indians Live in Tipis? Questions and Answers from the National Museum of the American Indian* (New York: HarperCollins, 2007).

5. Charles C. Mann, *1491: New Revelations of the Americas Before Columbus* (New York: Alfred A. Knopf, 2005), 332.

6. Andrea Smith, "Native American Feminism, Sovereignty and Social Change," *Feminist Studies* 31, no. 1 (Spring 2005): 132. See also Smith, *Conquest: Sexual Violence and American Indian Genocide* (Boston: South End Press, 2005), and Louise Erdrich, *The Round House* (New York: Harper, 2012). In *The Round House*, the 2012 National Book Award winner for fiction, Erdrich writes of the circumstances on reservations that allow for extreme sexual violence.

7. Amnesty International USA, *Maze of Injustice: The Failure to Protect Indigenous Women from Sexual Violence in the USA* (New York: Amnesty International USA, 2007).

8. Barker, *Native Acts*.

9. See Daniel M. Cobb, *Native Activism in Cold War America: The Struggle for Sovereignty* (Lawrence: University of Kansas Press, 2008).

10. The National Indian Youth Council (NIYC) continues in the twenty-first century, and Shirley Hill Witt is an active board member. For an excellent history of the NIYC, see Bradley G. Shreve, *Red Power Rising: The National*

Indian Youth Council and the Origins of Native Activism (Norman: University of Oklahoma Press, 2011).

11. Mishuana Goeman, *Mark My Words: Native Women Mapping Our Nations* (Minneapolis: University of Minnesota Press, 2013).

MYTH 20: "NATIVE AMERICANS CAN'T AGREE ON WHAT TO BE CALLED"

1. Harjo has long been known for her tireless work to bring awareness to issues of cultural appropriation in professional sports. In 2014 she was awarded the Presidential Medal of Freedom for her efforts, the highest civilian honor in the United States.

2. Peter d'Errico, "Native American Indian Studies: A Note on Names," Peter d'Errico's Law Page, http://www.umass.edu/legal/derrico/name.html.

3. Ibid.

4. It is for this reason that Indigenous scholars developed the framework known as "Fourth World" theory beginning in the 1970s. Referring to Indigenous peoples as "Fourth World" nations emphasizes their pre-state existence, making a distinction between the nation, as a bedrock community with deep and ancient connections to place, and the state, which is a legal construction that emerges out of the Treaty of Westphalia in 1648. It also deemphasizes the centrality of modern economics as the sole reference point inferred in the terms "First World" and "Third World." In other words, Indigenousness transcends both categories, which are incapable of recognizing the political existence of Indigenous peoples. See more generally Rudolph C. Rÿser, *Indigenous Nations and Modern States: The Political Emergence of Nations Challenging State Power* (New York: Routledge, 2012), and Rudolph Rÿser, Dina Gilio-Whitaker, and Heidi Bruce, "Fourth World Theory and Methods of Inquiry," in *Handbook on Indigenous Research Methodologies in Developing Nations*, ed. Patrick Ngulube, forthcoming 2016.

5. Lola García-Alix, *IWGIA Handbook: The Permanent Forum on Indigenous Issues* (Copenhagen: International Work Group for Indigenous Affairs, 2003).

6. Steven Newcomb, "From an Original Free Existence to an 'Indigenous' Existence," Indian Country Today Media Network, April 24, 2014, http://indiancountrytodaymedianetwork.com/2014/04/22/original-free-existence-indigenous-existence.

7. Amanda Blackhorse, "Blackhorse: Do You Prefer 'Native American' or 'American Indian'? 6 Prominent Voices Respond," Indian Country Today Media Network, May 21, 2015, http://indiancountrytodaymedianetwork.com/2015/05/21/blackhorse-do-you-prefer-native-american-or-american-indian-6-prominent-voices-respond.

MYTH 21: "INDIANS ARE VICTIMS AND DESERVE OUR SYMPATHY"

1. Theodore Roosevelt, *The Winning of the West: Part I: The Spread of English Speaking Peoples* (New York: Current Literature Publishing Company, 1905), 119, available on Internet Archive, https://archive.org/stream /winningofwest11roos#page/n5/mode/2up.

2. Even today's journalists can't resist the urge to invoke the trope of Indian plight, as exemplified in a 2014 British newspaper headline: Tom Payne, "President Obama Pledges to Improve the Plight of Poverty-Stricken Native Americans During Visit to Indian Reservation," *Independent*, June 14, 2014, http://www.independent.co.uk/news/world/americas/president -obama-pledges-to-improve-the-plight-of-poverty-stricken-native -americans-during-visit-to-9536999.html.

3. One of the more notorious examples comes from L. Frank Baum, author of the children's classic *The Wonderful Wizard of Oz*. He was also the editor of the *Saturday Pioneer* newspaper in Aberdeen, South Dakota, and in December 1890 and January 1891, on the heels of Hunkpapa Lakota leader Sitting Bull's murder and the Wounded Knee Massacre two weeks later, he published editorials calling for the "total annihilation" and "extermination" of the Indians. See Nancy Tystad Koupal, "The Wonderful Wizard of the West: L. Frank Baum in South Dakota, 1888–91," *Great Plains Quarterly* (January 1, 1989), http://digitalcommons.unl.edu/cgi/viewcontent.cgi?arti cle=1387&context=greatplainsquarterly.

4. Helen Hunt Jackson's *A Century of Dishonor* was reissued in 2003 with a subtitle, *The Classic Exposé of the Plight of the Native Americans*. Although this was not part of the original title, Jackson might well be credited with giving birth to the literary concept of the Indian plight.

5. It has been argued that despite the good intentions of Jackson's book, it was influential in Congress's passing of the 1887 Dawes Act, which ultimately proved disastrous for Indians. Some historians note that as flawed as the Dawes Act was, it was well-intentioned. However, congressional debates over the legislation revealed that some foresaw the devastating outcome and fought against it. Most notable was Senator Henry M. Teller from Colorado.

6. The Society of American Indians existed from 1911 to 1923, and even after its disbandment its former leaders continued their alliances with prominent white reformers such as John Collier, who founded the American Indian Defense Committee in 1923 and became commissioner of Indian affairs in 1933. See K. Tsianina Lomawaima, "The Society of American Indians," *American History*, Oxford Research Encyclopedias, http://american history.oxfordre.com/view/10.1093/acrefore/9780199329175.001.0001 /acrefore-9780199329175-e-31. See also Tom Holm, *The Great Confusion*

in Indian Affairs: Native Americans and Whites in the Progressive Era (Austin: University of Texas Press, 2005).

7. Lomawaima, "The Society of American Indians," 3.

8. Ibid., 8.

9. See Sherry L. Smith, *Hippies, Indians, and the Fight for Red Power* (Oxford, UK: Oxford University Press, 2012).

10. Ibid., 215.

11. Ibid., 217. The Twenty Point Position Paper was the creation of the American Indian Movement and carried with them during the Trail of Broken Treaties to Washington, DC, in 1972. The paper was a framework arguing for the strengthening of the treaty relationship and reinstatement of the treaty-making process, among other suggestions for improving the relationship between tribes and the federal government. Within the context of settler colonialism, it might be too optimistic to say that the spirit of the twenty points has prevailed, given that virtually none were ever adopted or even discussed by the Nixon administration. But Smith's point that things have generally improved in the relations between American Indians and the federal government since the termination years is well taken.

12. Ibid.

13. See Tim Baylor, "Media Framing of Movement Protest: The Case of American Indian Protest," *Social Science Journal* 33, no. 3 (1996): 241–55.

14. For a more in-depth discussion on measuring the success of social movements, see Dina Gilio-Whitaker, "Idle No More and Fourth World Social Movements in the New Millennium," *South Atlantic Quarterly* 114, no. 4 (2015): 866–78.

15. The famous "Baby Veronica" adoption is a case in point. A Cherokee father, Dusten Brown, had his daughter taken away from him after a 2013 Supreme Court decision ruled against him and for a non-Native adoptive couple based on the opinion that because the child had never lived with him before, he had no parental rights. Not only was it a severe blow to the Brown family, the precedent it set was an erosion of tribal sovereignty and weakening of the intent of the law.

16. The four Saskatchewan-based women are Nina Wilson, Sheela Mclean, Sylvia McAdam, and Jessica Gordon.

17. According to Chief Spence, chronic underfunding for essential human services like housing, water, sanitation, and education was an ongoing crisis that had finally reached a state of emergency, requiring drastic action.

18. Gilio-Whitaker, "Idle No More and Fourth World Social Movements in the New Millennium."

19. The demonstration was held in conjunction not only with the World Conference on Indigenous Peoples but also with a UN summit on climate

change the following day. According to the *Guardian*, the People's Climate March also coordinated marches in 161 other countries, with over half a million people participating. The paper reported that 310,000 people had flooded the streets of New York in the largest climate change march ever. Suzanne Goldenberg et al., "Climate Change Marches: Kerry Cites Fight Against Ebola and Isis as Thousands Join Protests," *Guardian*, September 22, 2014, http://www.theguardian.com/environment/2014/sep/21/-sp -climate-change-protest-melbourne-london-new-york-protest.

20. DiCaprio won the Golden Globe, as well as the Academy Award, for his role in *The Revenant*, which recalls the story of the frontiersman Hugh Glass and his struggle for survival in an uncharted North American wilderness.

21. Felix S. Cohen, "The Erosion of Indian Rights, 1950–53: A Case Study in Bureaucracy," *Yale Law Journal* 62 (1953): 349, 390.

22. Bolstering Robert Williams's research on the Supreme Court's racism in Indian cases, legal scholar Kathryn E. Fort has argued that by not exercising academic rigor in Native American cases, the court remains stuck in the past, lazily relying on histories that perpetuate the vanishing Native stereotype. See Fort, "The Vanishing Indian Returns: Popular Originalism and the Supreme Court," *Saint Louis University Law Journal* 57 (2013): 297.

23. Wanda D. McCaslin and Denise C. Breton, "Justice as Healing: Going Outside the Colonizers' Cage," in Denzin, Lincoln, and Smith, eds., *Handbook of Critical and Indigenous Methodologies*, 511–29.

HISTORICAL TIMELINE

1. See also Judith Nies, *Native American History: A Chronology of a Culture's Vast Achievements and Their Links to World Events* (New York: Ballantine Books, 1996).